GOOD, BE

THE
PASSIONATE
TOASTMASTER

Unleash Your Passion As A Communicator, Motivator, Storyteller & Humorist!

BY CRAIG HARRISON, DTM, AL, PDG

All Rights Reserved.

ISBN: 978-0-9825635-0-2

No part of this publication may be reprinted, reproduced, stored or transmitted by any means, electronic or mechanical, including photocopying, recording or by any information storage and retrieval system, without the prior written permission of the author.

Except for Toastmasters International® — identified information, products or services, all information, products and services referred to in this book are *not* official Toastmasters International documents or publications but are those of the author.

Cover photograph of Jolene Jang, A.K.A. the Fun Specialist (www.TheMeetingMaximizer.com) by Vinh Chung (www.MediaInMotion.com). Interview with Jeff Heidner reprinted by permission of Jeff Heidner. Photograph of Craig in Confidence, CA taken by Michael Harrison. Photograph of Craig and Michelle Gilstrap PDG by D-4's Robert Tang.

Published by Craig Harrison's
EXPRESSIONS OF EXCELLENCE! ™
3151 Eton Avenue, Suite 102, Berkeley, CA 94705
☞ **www.ConsummateToastmaster.com**
www.ExpressionsOfExcellence.com
www.VoiceOfCustomerService.com
www.CultivateTheLeaderInYou.com
www.HackinBoo.com
(510) 547-0664
Craig@ExpressionsOfExcellence.com

Praise for Craig's
GOOD, BETTER...BEST! Series

"Craig Harrison's speaking skills have found their match: his writing skills! His GOOD, BETTER...BEST! series is the Bible for every speaker. I wish I'd had these books when I started Toastmasters."

— Harvey Mackay, author of the New York Times #1 bestseller *Swim With the Sharks Without Being Eaten Alive*

* * * * * * * * * * *

"GOOD, BETTER...BEST! offers excellent tips and ideas for every level of Toastmaster, including speaking, storytelling, creativity, using humor, networking, managing meetings, sales, leadership, teamwork...inside—and outside— of our organization."

— Sheryl Roush, DTM, Past District Governor
Accredited Speaker, Sparkle Presentations, Inc.

* * * * * * * * * * *

"Craig Harrison *is* the ultimate Toastmaster. He has taken years of advice and study and made it understandable, digestible and practical. Anyone who is committed to going from GOOD to BETTER to BEST will find this a great investment of time. Why not benefit from Craig's years of speaking and leadership expertise?"

— Patricia Fripp, Certified Speaking Professional,
Speaker Hall of Fame
Cavett Award Recipient,
Past President, National Speaker Association

"Good, Better...Best! is a gold mine of information and inspiration for all Toastmasters by consummate Toastmaster Craig Harrison. I found these books a treat to read because of the easy-to-read style and the immense amount of useful information for Toastmasters of all experience levels. Craig's stories and examples add spice and impact to his points. Most of all, readers will find that this book is chockfull of easy-to-apply ideas to accelerate their personal growth. I especially appreciated the suggestions on how Toastmasters can apply their skills in the world. My sincere congratulations to Craig for writing this volume of great value to Toastmasters everywhere."

— Dilip Abayasekara, Ph.D., DTM
Accredited Speaker, Past International President

* * * * * * * * * * *

"A must read for all Toastmasters, both new and experienced! With a touch of humor and real-life examples, Craig has created a perfect how-to series to help anyone become the consummate Toastmaster. He explains simply what all Toastmasters need to know to become a consummate Toastmaster."

— Paula Tunison, Past International Director

* * * * * * * * * * *

"If you are going to do something, do it right! Craig's GOOD,BETTER...BEST! is a practical guide to becoming the absolute best Toastmaster you can be. Filled with useful information for both the club and workplace, Craig's book is a must read."

— Bo Bennett, host of "The Toastmasters Podcast" creator of FreeToastHost, author of *"Year To Success"*

"Good, Better…Best! is full of powerful, practical ideas that will enable both novice and experienced speakers to achieve their personal best. Through his use of personal examples, Craig brings his recommendations to life and shows how one can realize their full potential."

— Robert E. Barnhill, III, J.D., CPA/PFS, CFP®
Past International President, Toastmasters International®

* * * * * * * * * * * *

"In my more than ten years as a Toastmaster I have had the pleasure to enjoy the wit and wisdom of Consummate Toastmaster Craig Harrison's articles in *Toastmaster* magazine. This series compiles these articles into different categories that help the reader to become not only a better speaker and leader, but a Consummate Toastmaster. I highly recommend this book to learn from one of the best."

— Keith E Ostergard, DTM President & Chief Consultant
LPC Consulting, LLC
[凯瑞拓思企业管理顾问(北京)有限公司] Beijing, China

* * * * * * * * * * * *

"If you are dedicated to improving your communication and leadership skills, invest in yourself through buying and reading these books. Craig Harrison, a highly respected member of Toastmasters International — is a well-known author, motivational speaker and leader, committed to helping others."

— Ginger Kane, DTM, Past International Director

"Let Craig Harrison guide you to the confidence and influence you are capable of. Through this book series you will learn to optimize your Toastmasters experience."

— Jim Cathcart, CSP, CPAE
2001 Golden Gavel Recipient, Toastmasters International®

* * * * * * * * * * * *

"These practical and entertaining books are a read for not only Toastmasters (both "new" and "seasoned") but for all public speakers. GOOD, BETTER...BEST! is a treasure trove of practical advice written in a refreshing fun-to-read style. This could only have been written by a professional with extensive first-hand experience."

— Helen Blanchard, DTM
Toastmasters International President 1985-86
Author of *Breaking the Ice*

* * * * * * * * * * * *

"Craig Harrison is a Toastmasters sage! Craig has given to Toastmasters in every way imaginable: starting clubs, rescuing clubs, writing prolifically for *Toastmaster* magazine, and befriending Toastmasters from many countries in their home clubs, countless conferences and at International Conventions, inspiring them to be their best."

"In GOOD, BETTER...BEST! Craig has amassed a pragmatic collection of broad-based wisdom, a treasure trove of sparkling insights that we wish we knew, ideal for fledgling members as well as savvy leaders and emerging professional speakers, all vital reading. Happy Toastmastering!"

— Cassandra Cockrill, DTM District 57
President's Distinguished District Governor 2000-01

"Good, Better...Best! is an entertaining, insightful, and valuable foray into the world of Toastmasters. Toastmasters core values—integrity, excellence, respect for the invidivual, and service—thread their way through these excellent chapters."

— Tim Keck, Past International President,
Toastmasters International®

* * * * * * * * * * *

"Wow! What an incredible book series for Toastmasters and all those who aspire to excel in public speaking. As an international professional speaker myself and a Toastmaster for 20 years, I still learn new and powerful gems from this series. An interesting read, well illustrated with examples and great speaking tips. You will be learning volumes from Craig, the consummate communicator."

— Dr. YKK (Yew Kam Keong, Ph.D),
Chief Mindunzipper, Business innovation consultant,
Mindbloom Consulting, Sydney, Australia

* * * * * * * * * * *

"Using poetry, prose, humorous stories and poignant examples, Craig Harrison leaves no stone unturned as he lays out a blueprint for ultimate success for every Toastmaster. This volume is a must-read for anyone who desires to be a better Toastmaster and a better communicator. *Every* aspiring speaker *must* have this book."

— Mark L. Brown
World Champion of Public Speaking®
Presenter of the Emmy-nominated PBS Special
"Words Count with Mark Brown"

"Shave years off your learning curve by learning from a consummate teacher, Craig Harrison. Comprehensive, practical, and enjoyable, GOOD, BETTER...BEST! should be in every Toastmaster's library."

— David Brooks, DTM
1990 World Champion of Public Speaking

* * * * * * * * * * * *

"This book is obviously a work of love. Scholarly, yet practical as an everyday reference. Craig's empathy for and understanding of the human condition allows him to deliver overwhelming value to his audiences."

"Read this book. Study its principles.
And one day soon you will penetrate the veil between you and superb platform excellence."

— Burt Dubin, President, Personal Achievement Institute, Creator, *Speaker Success System*

* * * * * * * * * * * *

"Craig's GOOD, BETTER...BEST! series is a valuable resource for every speaker and Toastmaster: A desktop reference that will give you communication & leadership skills to super-charge your platform performance and energize your club."

— John Kinde, DTM, Accredited Speaker

* * * * * * * * * * * *

"If you value personal growth and the ability to lead others to new heights, then this is your book. Craig's books take Toastmasters to a whole new level."

— Dr. Vincent Muli Wa Kituku, Certified Speaking Professional

Table of Contents

I. TOASTMASTERING 1

    Introductions that Pave the Way To Winning Speeches 3

    Are You Listening to Your Audience? 13

    Unite and Conquer! Who's Your Audience? 18

    What About THEM? 28

    Your Speech's Closing: How Far Will You Go? 35

    Creative Strategies for Answering Table Topics 42

    Be a Creative Table TopicMaster 55

    Your Virtual Coaches: Let the Internet Become Your Co-Pilot 59

    How to Learn Customer Service as a Club Officer 67

II. MOTIVATION 73

    Turning Milestones Into Stepping Stones 75

    Greater Things to Come: Projecting Potential 81

    Finding Confidence 85

    Take Two: Value Derived From Serving a Second Time................ 88

III. HUMOR 91

    Speakers Say the Darndest Things 93

    A Funny Thing Happened On the Way to the Podium 97

    Toastmasters Do It...Until They Hear Applause 102

    How I Suffered from Foot-In-Mouth Disease 110

    Toastmasters Haikus 118

    The Communication Conundrum 123

    I Am Afraid To Speak.. 126

IV. STORYTELLING 131
Become a Storyteller… Two Minutes at a Time 133
Storytellers and Toastmasters: Learning from Each Other 138
Once Upon a Job: Success Stories Help Job Seekers
Sell Their Skills 144
Toastmaster Success Stories Reap Recruiting Rewards 149
From Silk to Story: Tellers and Toastmasters Trade Threads
of Traditions through Visit to China.. 151

V. EXCELLENCE 155
Expressions of Excellence 157
Good, Better…BEST! 163
Nine Ways to Improve Your Toastmasters Skills 169
How To Make Miss Manners Proud 171
Becoming the Consummate Toastmaster 176

VI. NEXT STEPS 181
What Now? 182
Taking it to the Streets... 187

VII. ABOUT YOUR AUTHOR.. 189
Craig Harrison the Toastmaster and Professional Speaker. 189
Other Resources of Craig's 191

Dedication

*This book series is dedicated
to the person who told me, repeatedly,
in the early 90's,
that I needed Toastmasters.*

*We joke that I would have joined sooner,
except for the fact that she told me to!*

*I'm referring of course to my Mother,
Evalee Harrison,
who taught and continues to teach me
much about communication.
Thank you mom for insisting, repeatedly,
that I needed to join Toastmasters.*

*Thank you for your patience
as I worked the various programs
Toastmasters has to offer for communication,
leadership and self-improvement.*

*And thank you for a lifetime's worth of
coaching, mentoring and nudging.*

Good, Better...BEST!

Acknowledgments

This book series would not be possible without the support, guidance and love of the many Toastmasters I've had the pleasure of working with since joining Lakeview Toastmasters in Oakland, CA, USA in 1992. Thank you Lakeview members past and present, including Julie Merrill, for bringing me in, Robert Cope and Ron Bishop for their love and tough love respectively, Ian McDonald, John Raphael, and Bill Young, the backbone of Lakeview Toastmasters. And a giant O for Orunamamu…The O is for Respect!

Thank you District 57 colleagues Ernest Villafranca, Barbara Branton, Anne Marie Levy, Adrian Levy, Whitnie Henderson, Mari Clark, Ed Stoermer, Parkman Joe, Nila Wong, Willie Mae Thomas, Lee Woods, Frank Santos, Shelley Lapkoff, Irma Rios, Bob Driscoll, Satya Sarkar, Vicky Lapp, Anupama Desai, Doreen Hamilton, Margie Hines, Monica Sullivan, Monica Wilcoxen, Leonard Edmondson, Joycelyn Myers-Farrow, Chuck Ward, Consuelo and Peter Hartman, Lindy Sinclair, Gary Wong DG and to colleagues no longer with us: Sid Levy, Asha Goldberg, John Cotter, Irene Monroe, Stephen Abbett, and Pamela McManus.

To Past District 57 Governors: Vivian Faye, Bill Meyn, Jim Doyle, Jr., Patrick McManus, Dennis Dubro, Tevis Thompson, Jr., Earleen Norris, Denise Abero, Al Mangarin, Judy Parrott, Kathy Todd Watson PID, Marion Keibel, Tyree Johnson and Ashley Harkness. Thank you past Toastmaster Michael J. Herman.

I've appreciated the support of District 4's past District Governors Margaret Fagetti, Dee Talley, Joe Madley and Susan Swope, Bob Hudak, and Bill Woolfolk PID, Point of Order members and Parliamentarians Kitty Mason PID, Accredited Speaker Wayne

Choate, Marilyn Collins, Ed Harley, Ezra Rosoff, Gregory M. Pribyl and Pro-Toasties leaders Aaron Ulysses Parnell, Kristy Rogers, Carolyn Millet, Chuck Eudy, John Harrison, Susan Schwartz and co-founders Shelly Horwitz and Cavett Award winner Patricia Fripp CSP, CPAE.

A special thank you to my Toastmasters mentor Ginger Kane PID and Max Kane DTM, and to Cassandra Cockrill PDG, my vision of the Consummate Toastmaster. Appreciation is also due to Second Vice-President Michael Notaro of City Center Toastmasters, PIDs Darleen Price, Feckry Ishmail and Paula Tunison, Marcia Hudgens, PDG Past International Presidents Tim Keck, Robert E. Barnhill III and Jana Barnhill.

I've been inspired by VJ Singal of District 56, Keith Ostergaard and Beijing #1 Toastmasters, the Tokyo Toastmasters club and Novocastrians of Newcastle, Australia, as well as the Lions Center for the Blind Toastmasters of Oakland, CA. World Champions of Public Speaking Morgan McArthur and Mark L. Brown have been particularly supportive, as have Accredited Speakers Anne Barab and the ever-sparkling Sheryl Roush, PDG.

I have the utmost admiration for the staff at World Headquarters, past and present. To the wonderful Suzanne Frey and her staff, executive director Daniel Rex, the late Terrence McCann, and to Stan Stills, David Kull, Debbie Horn Yosha and Nancy Langton: thank you for all your support of us as leaders and members of Toastmasters International.

I've been touched, moved and inspired by so many Toastmasters and clubs I've joined or started. Being unable to list you all by name, I simply say to each of you a heartfelt "Thank you." I strive to pay your lessons forward in my Toastmastering. —CH

Become A *Passionate* Toastmaster!

I. TOASTMASTERING

Attending and participating regularly in your club's meetings, accepting all roles and working your speech manuals will help you be a better Toastmaster.

This section will help you grow even further as a Toastmaster. It offers tips on researching your speech, constructing your speech introduction, gaining an audience-centered orientation and being inclusive in your speech's design and delivery. There are even ideas for becoming a better Table TopicsMaster and respondent.

Finally, there are tips on the value of serving in each club officer position. Read on!

Good, Better...BEST!

Introductions that Pave the Way To Winning Speeches

In baseball, the visiting team always bats first. Sometimes, the home team is already behind several runs, even before they come to bat for the first time.

As a speaker, I know the feeling. Recently I gave three speeches in one week. In each case, the introduction given by those in charge left me feeling as though I was "playing from behind" before I spoke my first word. While I eventually won over my audiences, I felt extra pressure to have a 'big inning' in order to prevail.

Let's face it; it's easy to strike out without the right person pitching your introduction.

Introductions Are Important

Audiences have needs. They need to know who is going to speak to them. They also want to know the speaker's topic. And they naturally wonder what qualifies the speaker to present this topic. What value does the presentation hold? Simply put, as listeners, they are asking, "What's in it for me?" They wish to know the benefits to be derived from listening to your speech.

That's a lot for you as a speaker to answer to, in addition to advancing your own message. The good news is your introducer can address the audience's questions, immediately and directly when you instruct him or her to do so. In fact, the introducer can do a better job than you can in accomplishing several of these objectives. Think of your introducer as a player you drafted especially to pitch your speech to an expectant, curious and sometimes skeptical audience in advance of your presentation.

The Starting Nine: Helping Your Introducer Score for You

Below are some guidelines for helping your introducer ace his or her role in setting the stage for you, the featured speaker.

1. Make sure your introduction is typed, in big print (such as an 18 point font). Use bold, italics or underline fonts strategically, though not excessively, to add emphasis and give additional guidance. AVOID ALL CAPS! They're harder to read and thus slower to read. If possible, keep your introduction to one page. The easier you make the introduction for your introducer, the better he can deliver it.

2. Spell complicated or foreign words phonetically to help your introducer pronounce them correctly. For example: if your name is Orunamamu, you might spell it OH-(pause) Roon-a-MAH-MOO. I recently had the pleasure of introducing John Eweglaben. It would have been so easy to pull an Ed McMahon, and simply say, "Here's Johnny!" Instead I had John spell his name out for me phonetically, and then practiced. Incidentally, it sounds like "A-wig-LAY-Bin." Try these:

   Osafran Okundaye — **Oh-sah-Fran A-kun-DĀY**

   Tony Bacezwski — **Tony Ba-SHEV-ski**

   Mademoiselle Carolyn Millet —
   Madam-MO-zell Carolyn Me-AAAAAAYE

3. Request that your introducer warm up in the bullpen before the first official pitch, so to speak. Ask her to read your introduction several times in advance, out loud, and then again *in your presence*. Introductions have their own rhythm, so it's important they are practiced out loud, not only silently, to achieve a conversational tone. Plus, you'll be able to correct any mistakes and give your introducer confidence that she is reading it properly.

4. Ask your introducer to honor your introduction by not ad-libbing. While many introducers think they are improving the introduction, often they bring in extraneous material or go on too long, confusing listeners with unneeded information. Explain that your introduction, as is, directly leads into your presentation, and that deviating from it will undermine your presentation's impact.

5. Work out details of the transfer. For example, how will you reach the stage or lectern? From what side will you arrive? Will you shake hands? Receive a microphone? (In which case the introducer might need to turn his microphone off.) Assume control of theirs? (In this case, thank them for NOT turning theirs off before handing it to you.) Will you be carrying props? Give your introducer cues so he or she can assist you and not detract from your impact.

6. Make sure your introduction has the basics: your name, business title if appropriate, and the title of your talk.

7. Do you want your introducer to lead applause at the end of their introduction? If so, remind them in writing. Are there jokes within the introduction? If so, instruct them to laugh as a way of insuring the audience knows that it's OK to laugh. Are pauses

critical to the timing of your introduction? If so, spell them out and consider placing them in brackets so the introducer knows to honor them. For example: [pause for laughter.]

8. You know best what tone you wish your introduction to set for your speech. Let your introducer know! Are you trying to signal a good time ahead? Or do you wish to start on a somber or serious note? Use cues in your introduction to support your preferred tone. For example, if your introduction signals something serious, you might ask the introducer to deliver some lines softly [whisper] or to demarcate key points in a deliberate fashion [pause here for emphasis]. Important items may be <u>underlined</u> or **emboldened**.

9. Just as a batting practice pitcher sacrifices his arm to warm up batters on his own team, so too should your introducer warm up or loosen up the audience. If interaction is desired, let the introducer know that questions in the introduction are not rhetorical but require an audience response. For instance, "Are you following me?" *[Now pause for audience reaction!]* (If this sentence is followed by silence from the audience, it should be asked again by the introducer, more loudly and expectantly.)

Stuck in the On-Deck Circle

Some introducers forget that they are there to enhance your presentation. They may be under the (mistaken) impression that they are the focal point and their banter is more important than your introduction. Others are so enamored of hearing their own voice they forget to welcome yours. More than once, I've waited side-stage while a loquacious emcee or introducer droned on, putting the audience to sleep and eating up valuable stage time.

Curves Cross Up Your Receiver

Every once in a while, a catcher will call for a certain pitch and, through miscommunication or defiance, the pitcher will deliver, say, a curveball when a fastball was called. More than not receiving the pitch requested, the change of pace can disrupt the timing of the team. So, too, with introductions.

Once I was to be introduced by a colleague I had known in a previous organization. This actually comforted me, as my presentation was to be videotaped that day and I was looking forward to his smooth, effective and heartfelt introduction. As usual, I had sent my typed, one-page introduction to my friend the emcee well in advance, and was waiting side-stage to be introduced.

Imagine my surprise when my friend ad-libbed to discuss how long he'd known me, what he thought of my hometown's politics, and how he once met my mother. Not only did he dilute the intended impact of my well-crafted introduction, he used up valuable time and compromised my videotape. Whether well intended or just self-indulgent, introducers sometimes balk when asked to deliver our pitch "straight as she flies."

Batting Cleanup

There have been times I have been over-introduced. You'd have thought I cured cancer, won the Second World War, and was the first man on the moon. While we all like to receive well-deserved praise, sometimes our credibility is actually undermined by being oversold.

Now Pitching...

Once I was introduced with the statement "Craig is a professional speaker, he can speak on any topic!" While not wanting to embarrass or contradict my introducer, I was more proud of the fact that I only speak within my area of expertise when outside Toastmasters, the true mark of a professional. I nicely clarified my introducer's remarks to regain some credibility and focus on my true strengths.

Another time I was introduced as the person who had built several Toastmasters clubs the audience knew. My introducer had done his own research and overstated my contributions. I chose not to correct him at the time, yet later was assailed by others in the audience for appearing to take credit for their work.

Remember, as a leader from the platform you have an obligation to be accurate, truthful and correct, whether in your language, facts or the overall presentation of your speech and yourself. Since my presentation was on leadership that day, I missed an opportunity to set the record straight and share recognition with those who had done the work. Error: Speaker!

Know Your Role

When planning your introduction, know your spot in the rotation. Are you batting leadoff, the first speaker at a daylong conference? If so your introduction can set the tone for the entire day.

Are you setting the table for ensuing speakers? Your audience may be there to hear Zig Ziglar, Jeanne Robertson or Jim

Cathcart, and not you, so tailor your introduction accordingly. Are you the main event? If so, your introduction may differ from that of an opening act or warm-up speaker. Develop an appreciation for the differences.

Humor and Humility

Some speakers instruct their introducers to cite their various awards, degrees and accomplishments, whether or not they relate to the presentation at hand. Their intent is to establish credibility, and thus respect, from their audiences. This practice is important, to a point. Try not to overwhelm your audience with all your credentials. Show your good taste by picking awards and accomplishments that are most relevant to your speech or credibility and let the rest go.

The real way to garner respect from audiences is to use humor and some humility. Sometimes haughty credentials, instead of impressing an audience, build a wall between the speaker and the listeners. Use of humor, humility and even some self-effacement shows audiences that you are one of them, struggling with the same issues and challenges as they are. That's endearing. Give the audience reasons to like you, and they surely will.

At an event full of accomplished speakers with numerous degrees and certifications, one speaker was introduced as having her MHR. Her introducer paused to await reaction, yet there was none. Later the speaker hearkened back to her introduction and explained that they, in the audience, were also MHRs. She informed everyone that the MHR she possessed meant she was a Member of the Human Race. She combined humor and humility to endear herself to her audience. That's a two-run homer!

Foreshadowing with your Introduction

Often your introduction can set up a running joke, plant the seeds for a future story or scene, or introduce a theme to be revisited throughout your presentation.

Just as the catcher will throw back the ball to the pitcher after a pitch, many times the speaker acknowledges his or her introducer immediately following their appearance. For instance, after a funny introduction, the humorist might add "I'd like to thank Barbara for her gracious remarks. I started to get nervous when I heard all the accolades. I thought perhaps she was introducing a different speaker! Thanks Barbara, and your check's in the mail."

The Designated Hitter

Tony Brigmon, a longtime professional speaker, always brings his introducer with him. Knowing that introducing speakers isn't everyone's strong suit, Tony gives meeting planners an option. When it's time for Tony's speech, the emcee announces that a personal friend of Tony's has asked to introduce him. Then a man who looks a great deal like Tony comes up on stage and begins the introduction. "It's a pleasure to introduce Tony Brigmon of Grand Prairie, Texas. Heck, I've known him all my life. What a nice guy, a caring individual and a gem to listen to. You'll notice him right away, when he comes out he often waves his hands like this. Now, please give a warm welcome to Tony Brigmon!"

And then the introducer (who we know as Tony), walks backstage, pauses a minute, and then comes back onstage waving wildly to an adoring audience. Tony's already scored humor points with his creative introduction (of himself).

A Pitch in Time...

Just remember this, you can hit a home run whether you're pitched a fastball, curve ball or knuckle ball. While your introduction can help or hinder you, ultimately it's just your introduction. You've still got the power to connect with your audience, score points with listeners and win them over to your point of view. You can make every audience feel like the hometown fans with a well-designed introduction. Are you ready? Batter up!

Note to readers: See next page for an sample introduction, annotated with notes for the introducer, and for you, the reader, to understand how it was constructed.

Actual introduction is 8.5 x 11" and uses 16-pt or 18-pt type for ease of reading by novice introducers who are easily unnerved.

Good, Better...BEST!

SAMPLE INTRODUCTION

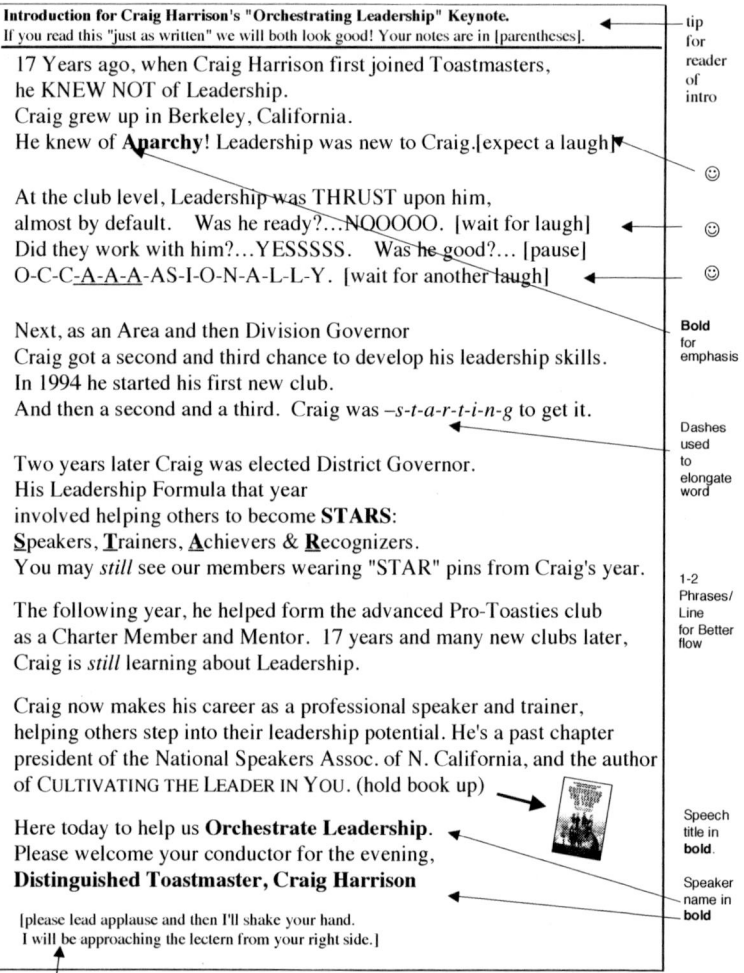

Introduction for Craig Harrison's "Orchestrating Leadership" Keynote.
If you read this "just as written" we will both look good! Your notes are in [parentheses]. ← tip for reader of intro

17 Years ago, when Craig Harrison first joined Toastmasters,
he KNEW NOT of Leadership.
Craig grew up in Berkeley, California.
He knew of **A**narchy! Leadership was new to Craig.[expect a laugh] ☺

At the club level, Leadership was THRUST upon him,
almost by default.   Was he ready?...NOOOOO. [wait for laugh] ☺
Did they work with him?...YESSSSS.   Was he good?... [pause]
O-C-C-<u>A-A-A</u>-AS-I-O-N-A-L-L-Y. [wait for another laugh] ☺

Next, as an Area and then Division Governor   **Bold**
Craig got a second and third chance to develop his leadership skills.   for emphasis
In 1994 he started his first new club.
And then a second and a third. Craig was –s-t-a-r-t-i-n-g to get it.
                                                Dashes used to elongate word

Two years later Craig was elected District Governor.
His Leadership Formula that year
involved helping others to become **STARS**:
Speakers, **T**rainers, **A**chievers & **R**ecognizers.   1-2 Phrases/ Line for Better flow
You may *still* see our members wearing "STAR" pins from Craig's year.

The following year, he helped form the advanced Pro-Toasties club
as a Charter Member and Mentor. 17 years and many new clubs later,
Craig is *still* learning about Leadership.

Craig now makes his career as a professional speaker and trainer,
helping others step into their leadership potential. He's a past chapter
president of the National Speakers Assoc. of N. California, and the author
of CULTIVATING THE LEADER IN YOU. (hold book up)

Here today to help us **Orchestrate Leadership**.   Speech title in **bold**.
Please welcome your conductor for the evening,
Distinguished Toastmaster, Craig Harrison   Speaker name in **bold**

[please lead applause and then I'll shake your hand.
I will be approaching the lectern from your right side.]

Tip for introducer: Introduction is written to help the Introducer succeed. Sentences are broken into phrases with commas acting as pauses for the Introducer and audience to breathe and digest what has been said.

Are You Listening to Your Audience?

As speakers we naturally believe that our audiences should listen to us. But how well are we listening to them? Believe it or not, that's the key to really connecting with an audience.

It may surprise you to learn that your audience speaks. I don't mean the whispering and side conversations that may occur during your speech. I mean the feedback they give you, the speaker, with facial expressions, body posture and attentiveness, throughout your presentation. Applause isn't the only time you can "listen" to your audience.

Listen *Before* You Speak

Prior to being introduced for your presentation, what do you hear from the audience? Are they restless, listless, or something in between? Are the people in the back making noise, the people in the sunlight getting drowsy? Has the previous speaker or activity lulled them into a state of complacency? Are they already psyched up from a previous discussion or interchange?

I've been at club meetings where a provocative business meeting has left people on edge, or when a spirited table topics session left members upbeat. Once my speech followed a hypnotherapist. I just wish she'd restored our members to their "original upright position."

Take the tenor of your audience before you approach the podium. Note their state. You may wish to alter your remarks or the way you deliver them to better connect with your audience.

You can even tell your introducer to "rev the audience up" a little more if they are down, or to tone down your introduction if your audience is already flying high and your topic requires serious reflection.

Be "In the Moment"

Most speakers I know prepare extensively, even visualizing their speech opening prior to arriving at the podium. Yet, when you are introduced and look out at your actual audience, you should not be completely on autopilot. Take a moment to gauge your audience's mood as you look out at them.

I've seen a speaker ask everyone to take a breath or two with him, so they could all begin refreshed. Similarly, I've seen speakers, as a change of pace, ask their audiences to close their eyes for a moment while the speaker paints a scene in their mind's eye. This breaks any spell that lingered from a previous speaker or activity. I've asked audiences who have been sitting too long to stand up and take a fifteen second stretch break with me.

Sending and Receiving Information

Speaking isn't just a 'stand and deliver' proposition. Speaking involves receiving information as well. Has your audience been properly predisposed to your presentation through the way you were introduced? Did members laugh or "ooh" or "ah" where you intended them to during your own opening? Can they hear you? Can they see you?

By "listening" to your audience you can determine whether all members of your audience can hear you, whether people in the back as well as the front can see you, and also whether your audience is tracking your presentation in other ways.

How do the faces of your audience look? Are they relaxed? Are they nodding in agreement? Are they leaning forward, indicating they either can't hear you or are having trouble understanding you?

If you are using highly technical terms, speaking at a fast rate of speed, or possess a thick accent, your audience members may be expending additional effort to understand your speech and follow your train of thought. You may "hear" this from furrowed brows or members turning to each other to ask "what did she say?" or "what does that mean?" That's you cue to clarify your statements, slow down or strive to enunciate more clearly. Often, due to time constraints, we over-rely on TLAs (three letter acronyms) or jargon. Sometimes, we just try to say too much in a short period of time. Especially in speeches, less is more.

Try to decipher what you "hear" from your audience, what it means, and then what you can do about it. When the audience is fidgeting, they may be too hot. (That's easy; lower the temperature in the room.)

Or, is their fidgeting due to other causes, perhaps your topic or subject matter? In that case, especially if this reaction is unintended, acknowledge what you see. Avoid "making your audience wrong" for their feelings or reactions to your presentation. They have a right to react in any way they wish. Perhaps you're touching a nerve. Your listening lets you know.

Some speakers will unintentionally divide their audience through their presentation. Whether you're competing in a contest or just trying to persuade your audience of your point of view, dividing your audience through polarizing remarks can undermine your efforts. Remarks that praise one group at another's expense leave part of your audience feeling smart, the other just smarting from your remarks. Strive to speak to universal themes or find the common ground within your diverse audience for maximum success.

Sound Advice on Humor

It's said that humor is invoked for one of three purposes: as a shield to protect, as a sword to attack, or as a bridge to connect. Listen to your audience's response to determine if your humor is bringing your audience together, unifying and connecting them. If your humor is falling flat, you may be dividing your audience through humor that is only funny to part of the group: women or men, young or old, etc. Strive to use humor that all can revel in.

Another important key to humor: give your audience time to laugh! Use pauses to allow your humor to sink in. Your pauses send cues to your audience that they are encouraged to ponder your words, and react accordingly. If they aren't laughing, it may be because you're not allowing them the opportunity to laugh. Take a breath now and then and watch the laughter flow.

For those competing in contests, realize that the larger the audience you speak to, the longer the audience takes to laugh. Don't get disqualified because your 7 minute speech at the club level goes 7 minutes fifteen seconds at the Area Contest and then at the Division level laughter pushes its time to seven and three quarters of a minute. Plan accordingly so you can listen to your audience's laughter without losing control of your speech's timing.

Giving Your Audience a Place in Your Presentation

Without an audience, you're just talking to yourself. Make sure your presentation has a place in it for them, and not just through their laughter. Members of your audience want and need to be a part of your presentation. They need to be acknowledged. They enjoy being involved and respect a speaker who respects them.

Help your audience find themselves within your presentation. Listen for opportunities for them to respond, react and be recognized and you will be hear thunderous applause by speech's end. Whether you address certain members by name, acknowledge specifics of their experience, or reference previous events in the room, such customization within your presentation shows you've been listening, looking and learning about them and their experience. Audiences love that!

So the next time you speak to an audience, don't forget to listen to them, too. They'll hear you better when you do!

Unite and Conquer!
Who's Your Audience?

Most speakers desire to win over audiences in their entirety. Who wouldn't want unanimous approval, a standing ovation and all the advantages that accrue from a successful speech?

Yet more times than not, speakers sabotage themselves in their quest to connect. Sometimes, they don't realize they've divided, alienated or even polarized an audience through ill-conceived remarks or lack of sensitivity. The results: lukewarm receptions, sparse applause and in the case of contests, a seat outside the winner's circle.

Assumptions, Presumptions

Often, speakers presume audiences think as they do or share their belief systems, values or political preferences. They arrive at this conclusion because the audience members look like they do, or because in their city, town or region, most people do share their beliefs. But often looks belie reality. You may be able to ascertain the gender of audience members by sight, but you can't see under people's skin. You cannot see inside their hearts or minds. Thus, when you presume, you run the risk of offending, if not insulting, audience members without even knowing it.

I've listened to speeches where the speaker presumed everyone in the room voted for the same candidate in the most recent national or local election, or that everyone in the club shared his belief about an upcoming holiday, or her stance on a war or domestic policy. Upon further review, it turned out there was anything but unanimity of opinion among the audience. Those holding divergent views from the speaker were less than 100% receptive to the speaker because the speaker presumed he or she spoke for everyone. Not so!

Speaking In the Lion's Den

Sometimes we find ourselves speaking to an audience with different beliefs, perspectives or experiences. In the United States you might be:

- ❖ A lone Republican speaking to an audience of Democrats, or vice versa
- ❖ A manager speaking to employees
- ❖ A Northerner speaking in the deep South
- ❖ A woman speaking to an all-male audience

Internationally, you may find yourself across a fence from an audience because you are:

- ❖ A Muslim speaking to a Christian audience, or vice versa
- ❖ An Aborigine speaking to Australians of English heritage
- ❖ A Korean speaking to a largely Japanese audience
- ❖ A Ghanaian addressing a predominantly Nigerian audience

In each case, there may be differing customs, values and even accents. To ignore such differences would be like ignoring an elephant in the room. The lack of acknowledgement would distract from your actual message. The wise approach is to acknowledge differences in a respectful way.

Inclusivity

Think for a moment about the way Toastmasters often open their speeches: "Mister/Madame Toastmaster, Fellow Toastmasters and Most Welcome Guests." This opening is designed to include and welcome everyone in your audience. That's good!

Similarly, we want to cast a wide net when speaking to audiences who may be skeptical, doubtful or reluctant to embrace our message because of their own background, disposition or past experiences. Craft your opening to engage all, especially those who may be in the minority in terms of gender, religion, age, political preference, etc.

Reputations Help and Hinder

I grew up and continue to reside in Berkeley, CA, home of the University of California along with the free speech movement, protests and riots of the 1960's. Was I a part of the riots of the 60s? I was seven years old. I was busy selling lemonade on the corner like any child of my age. Yet some audiences presume people from Berkeley are long-haired hippies who are rebels, radicals and draft dodgers with no respect for authority. Some dislike me before I've spoken a word, based on Berkeley's reputation. That's why I dispel their fears with humor and self-effacement in my speech's introduction.

The Elephant in the Room

Speechwriter Tom Roberts of Oakland, California hails from Arkansas, where as a college professor he taught public speaking, oral interpretation, broadcast journalism. Audiences always have two questions for Tom: "Why don't you sound like you're from the South?" And "Do you know President Bill Clinton?" After 17 years as a national broadcaster Tom has trimmed his regional accent. Yet, his credentials still color his audience's first impressions. Tom anticipates the questions and answers them at the outset to refocus his audiences.

Dynamic professional speaker Mikki Williams of Chicago, with her big hair and big jewelry, has audiences pondering a resemblance Barbara Streisand, Laynie Kazan or Bette Midler. Knowing this, at the outset, she eggs the audience on with "OK, who do I look like?" She vogues a little and the audience shouts out names. In her speaking school, Mikki coaches all speakers to "go with the obvious. Call on your attributes. If you're bald, pregnant or have a pronounced accent, reference it. Use self-directed humor to connect with your audience." If you're vertically challenged you might open with "Can you see me now?" Then, stand on your tiptoes and ask again!

Blues musicians Howlin' Wolf and Willie Dixon long ago taught that "you can't judge a book by lookin' at its cover." Initially, however, that is all audience members have to go on. Your mission, if you choose to accept it, is to help audiences get to know, trust and like you through your graciousness, inclusive engagement and appropriate disclosures. Especially at the beginning of your speech, these qualities help you bond with an audience that, as a result, will see you as more alike than different from them.

What presumptions do you possess about people from certain regions, of other religions, a certain age or orientation? What presumptions might people have of you, based solely by your age, gender, ethnicity, orientation or occupation? Accurate or not, these ideas affect how you are heard, seen and perceived. It also affects how you, as speaker, see and perceive your audience.

The Olive Branch

The best speeches are inclusive, bringing audiences together or offering something for multiple perspectives, beliefs or preferences. In cases where you are speaking to a hostile or opposition party, praise them! It will disarm them. When you are conciliatory or otherwise generous with your acknowledgement, their respect for you grows. By being magnanimous, you show yourself to be worthy of further consideration.

A Toast to Differing Tastes

A great, if exaggerated, example of catering to multiple factions within an audience can be found in the famous "whisky" speech of Judge Noah S. "Soggy" Sweat Jr. Delivered to the Mississippi legislature on April 4, 1952, this speech takes a stand on the controversial prohibition topic of legalizing liquor (then illegal in that state). In successive paragraphs, he appears to be either pummeling or praising the effects of alcohol. He seemingly appealed to both sides while maintaining his neutrality. (See sidebar.)

Whiskey Sour or Whiskey Sweet?

THE "WHISKEY" SPEECH, given by Judge Noah S. "Soggy" Sweat Jr. on April 4, 1952 to the Mississippi legislature:

"My friends,
"I had not intended to discuss this controversial subject at this particular time. However, I want you to know that I do not shun controversy. On the contrary, I will take a stand on any issue at any time, regardless of how fraught with controversy it might be. You have asked me how I feel about whiskey. All right, here is how I feel about whiskey."If when you say whiskey you mean the devil's brew, the poison scourge, the bloody monster, that defiles innocence, dethrones reason, destroys the home, creates misery and poverty, yea, literally takes the bread from the mouths of little children; if you mean the evil drink that topples the Christian man and woman from the pinnacle of righteous, gracious living into the bottomless pit of degradation, and despair, and shame and helplessness, and hopelessness, then certainly I am against it.

"But;
"If when you say whiskey you mean the oil of conversation, the philosophic wine, the ale that is consumed when good fellows get together, that puts a song in their hearts and laughter on their lips, and the warm glow of contentment in their eyes; if you mean Christmas cheer; if you mean the stimulating drink that puts the spring in the old gentleman's step on a frosty, crispy morning; if you mean the drink which enables a man to magnify his joy, and his happiness, and to forget, if only for a little while, life's great tragedies, and heartaches, and sorrows; if you mean that drink, the sale of which pours into our treasuries untold millions of dollars, which are used to provide tender care for our little crippled children, our blind, our deaf, our dumb, our pitiful aged and infirm; to build highways and hospitals and schools, then certainly I am for it

"This is my stand. I will not retreat from it. I will not compromise."

— Noah S. "Soggy" Sweat Jr.

Appealing to Our Commonalities

When speaking to audiences who appear to be different from you, seek that which you have in common and build upon that. For instance, you may be speaking to an audience comprised predominantly of those whose political beliefs are opposite to yours, and this is known to all. Your opening greeting may begin "Good evening friends and fellow citizens…" In theory you are all citizens. Other things you may have in common: you are all taxpayers, voters and survivors of that evening's Chicken à la Firestone. Look for common ground to launch your speech, and you and your audience will start the journey together.

When you speak to audiences from other countries, take the time to learn enough of their language to welcome them and help them feel at home. Whether you are using sign language for the deaf or colloquialisms, or dressing the part through a hat, tie, scarf or other sartorial garnishes, you are embracing the audience for who they are, and they will appreciate it, when it's done with sincerity.

Lisa Jeffery, a Miami Beach, Florida speech professor, corporate trainer and coach gives this example. "Consider a female health care professional speaking to Baptist ministers on the controversial topic of abortion. She's got to start out on common ground. Likability is important. She should strive to garner some 'amen's' early in her speech through praise, respect and a focus on that which is shared by the speaker and audience… Otherwise cognitive dissonance intercedes." Lisa coaches her clients and students to focus on achievable goals. In this case, getting the ministers to open their minds to a divergent point of view may be attainable. Converting them to change their belief system, through her speech alone, is far less likely.

For the Benefit of a Few

Many times in a speech you may speak about an event, experience or phenomenon that most, but not everyone knows, understands or is familiar with.

Consider the phrase "blue moon." Don't assume everyone knows it, or worse yet, ask in a condemning way, "Is there anyone here who doesn't know what a 'blue moon' is?" Instead, explain if for all: "...for those of you unfamiliar with expression 'once in a blue moon,' it refers to the second moon in a month, a rare occurrence." That way you don't embarrass, demean or ostracize the person who doesn't understand or hasn't been versed in your history, points of reference or colloquialism. Few people wish to admit in a crowd that they don't understand something. Yet it may inhibit their ability (or desire) to follow your speech, embrace your argument or support your cause.

Insights on Inside Jokes

Another way speakers alienate their audiences is through excessive use of "inside jokes" or references to events or knowledge known by some—but not most—of the audience. Your goal is to help everyone feel like an insider. Too many insider references estrange the listener from the speaker. Help people feel included, not excluded. There's little satisfaction in feeling you're in the "out" group when listening to a speaker.

Speak to Win!

Professional speaker Simma Lieberman of Berkeley, CA is known as *The Inclusionist*. She trains organizations worldwide in how to succeed through inclusion. Simma knows the value of helping audiences feel better about themselves. She says, "To be an inclusive speaker means that you know how to create community in the short time you are in front of people, by engaging them and making them feel like you are talking to (all of) them." She goes to great efforts to learn as much about her audience as possible. Beforehand she asks questions. Then she greets them upon arrival and uses questions in her opening remarks to engage and include everyone. As a result, she wins their attention, respect and adoration.

You can too! When you unite your audience the applause will be unanimous!

To summarize, keep these pointers in mind when speaking to a new group:

Tips for Better Knowing Your Audience

- ❖ Learn about your audience before you speak. Ask questions, meet them informally, use polls, surveys and questionnaires.

- ❖ Meet your audience members on their way into the room. Chat with them one-on-one and in small groups to learn more about them, identify commonalities.

- Use the African technique of "Call and Response" to engage and include your audience. "How many of you have children? (Wait for response.) How many of you ARE children?" (Wait for laughter!)
- Include your audience through generous eye contact that demonstrates you see them as individuals.
- Within your audience, speak to a person in the front, in the middle, and the back; speak to people on the left, to the right, in the center. Alternate where you direct your remarks.
- Remember, the shortest distance between people is often a smile. When you smile at someone, they usually smile back.
- If you're from out of town, reference something local about the town, region or state.
- Topical references often connect you with your audience. Mention the local weather (which we all experience), the traffic jam on the way to the program, a recent event, etc.
- Remember, you're not a speaker without an audience. They are the most valuable people in the room. Speaking is a collaborative experience. Share the spotlight with them and they'll respond appreciatively!
- Embrace humor that derives naturally from the room, audience, setting, etc. Sometimes the best humor is accidental or originates from audience members. Indulge and embrace this form of co-created magic.

What About THEM?

How to be an Audience-Centered Speaker When Speaking Beyond Toastmasters

When I first began speaking, I had stories to tell and it didn't matter who I told them to. And so I gave speeches in clubs, at contests and even beyond Toastmasters. I spoke about whatever was on my mind and paid little mind to who was in my audience, their background or needs.

It was only as I became an advanced speaker and began speaking, outside of Toastmasters, for a fee that I understood how important it is to consider my audience and their needs. This has made me a better speaker, and also better received.

We've all heard people give the same speech repeatedly, with little regard for the difference in audiences. One of the earliest lessons I learned in Toastmasters was that the same speech doesn't garner the same response when it's given at another club, at a contest or outside Toastmasters. Now I understand: each audience is different.

What Is An Audience?

Any time you speak to a group of people, they are considered an audience. Audiences are both a collection of individuals with their own needs and wants and an entity in its own right. It can be said that an audience is greater than the sum of its parts.

In Toastmasters, your audience is predominantly other Toastmasters, people who will clap out of courtesy before and after your speech, however good, relevant or useful your presentation. They also value certain qualities: a well organized presentation, good vocal variety, effective eye contact and appropriate body gestures. If your speech is full of um's and ah's, is read from notes and goes over its time limit, you will not have met the standards Toastmasters hold in high regard.

What Do You Know About Them?

When you speak to a non-Toastmasters group, different standards prevail. Your key to success in these situations comes from understanding the audience's standards and expectations. What do you know about your audience?

Here are some questions to ask yourself before speaking outside of Toastmasters. Answer them and prepare for success.

Why are they there?

We know from experience that there's a difference between attending by choice or out of duty and obligation. Traffic school is a perfect example of an audience that doesn't want to be there.

Determine your audience's motivation in attending. Is it voluntary? Compulsory? Are they paying with their own money or the company's money? Only when you understand their motivation can you truly fulfill their expectations.

What do they know?

An audience that doesn't know your topic or your lexicon may have trouble following you, or lack the desire to do so. We often assume our audience members know facts and share points of reference of ours.

Many members of audiences these days were born outside the U.S., or more recently than we were. You can't assume kids today know the bands Paul McCartney or George Michaels once played with, or even that U.S. President George W. Bush's father was also a U.S. President. Gauging your audience's knowledge is important.

What don't they know?

Audiences may not have your sense of history, or share your technical background. If you use big words, they may politely nod to obscure their embarrassment in not understanding you.

When in doubt, try not to talk "over the head" of your audience. Conversely, try not to "talk down" to your audience. Audiences lose respect for speakers who don't respect their intelligence.

What do they believe?

We often assume others are like us, whether politically, religiously or in other ways. When looking out at an audience you can't tell whether they're from the South, East or Far East, or about their lifestyle or personal beliefs.

Many a speaker has assumed, mistakenly, that their audience shared his or her values, beliefs and desires and either misjudged, or worse, offended their listeners. Respect your audience by striving to understand their beliefs. Even if you don't embrace them, understanding them allows you to accord them the proper respect they deserve as audience members.

What do they value?

What values does your audience cherish? Each audience is different. When I speak at Habitat for Humanity events, I know that attendees hold dear the American dream of owning one's home. When I speak to entrepreneurs, I understand they believe in the values of initiative and risk taking. Rotarians are steeped in their four questions: Is it the truth? Is it fair to all concerned? Will it build goodwill and better relationships? Will it be beneficial to all concerned?"

Knowing what an audience values helps you tailor your presentation to better resonate with them.

What are their sacred cows?

Beware of that which your audience holds sacred. I've watched non-Toastmasters disregard time limits, use inappropriate language and in other ways fly in the face of our speaking conventions.

Knowing what your audiences hold sacred allows you to decide whether to "steer" clear or milk their prized beliefs! The quickest way to alienate an audience is to mock or disparage that which they hold sacred. Wherever you speak, tread lightly or proceed at your own risk!

What's funny to them?

When your sense of humor matches your audience's, you score big points. Find out what's funny to them. Some audiences like gallows humor, many do not. Most audiences like touching human-interest stories, a few find them schmaltzy. Slapstick or non-verbal humor may actually play better than humorous stories for some audiences.

It's not what you find funny that matters; it's what makes your audience laugh.

What's *not* funny to them?

Beware of jokes. In speeches, jokes generally aren't as well received as humorous stories. (Jokes have a recognizable format, a clear punch line and less description than a humorous story.)

Also beware of telling lawyer jokes to attorneys, doctor jokes to physicians, etc. At best, they've heard them before and can tell them better than you!

Here's How You Do It!

Advanced research of an audience can really help you connect during your presentation. Using a pre-speech survey, observing the group with other speakers or even interviewing members by phone, e-mail or in person before you speak to their group can all help you to connect during your presentation.

Also, use your keen observation skills during your presentation to build solid rapport, trust and mutual appreciation. Below are seven habits of highly successful speakers that are useful speaking to outside audiences:

Tips to win over a non-Toastmasters audience

- ❖ Do your research in advance so as to customize your remarks, examples and visuals if applicable.
- ❖ Praise your audience sincerely near the beginning of your presentation.
- ❖ Speak to them with respect throughout.
- ❖ Be gracious.
- ❖ Be humble.
- ❖ Roll with the punches when unexpected things happen.
- ❖ Use self-effacing humor to connect with them.

Bear in mind when you speak to a non-Toastmasters audience that they are not only forming an opinion of you, but of Toastmasters too You are on display even before and after your official presentation, so be mindful that all eyes as well as ears are upon you as you arrive, socialize and dine in seemingly "off-stage" settings.

Place your audience at the center of your focus when preparing your outside presentations. By being audience-centered you will make a great first impression and a lasting impression as well.

Your Speech's Closing: *How Far Will You Go?*

In my seventeen years as a Toastmaster, I've heard over 2,000 speeches: Ice Breakers, contest winners and every other variety of speech from our Communication & Leadership and advanced speech manuals. They've covered myriad topics and encompassed a slew of styles.

And yet most of them share a common trait, and it isn't the presence of um's and ah's. It's that THEY DIDN'T GO FAR ENOUGH! They went plenty long, but most didn't go far enough. They closed with a whimper, not a bang!

An attorney culminates a case with a powerful closing argument. An opera ends with fanfare. Yet many speeches just quietly fade away or limp to an end. They leave us wanting more. They often miss an opportunity to emphatically drive home their points. Why don't these speakers "seal the deal?"

Are they afraid? Unsure? Are they uncomfortable coming on too strong? Or is it that they just don't realize how powerful they truly are?

The Speaking Formula: A Four-Part Equation

In any speech there are four components: the speaker, the audience, the speech and its result.

THE SPEAKER has a point of view, an opinion or a belief he or she endeavors to express. There's a purpose for speaking.

THE AUDIENCE is usually open to hearing from the speaker and willing to listen to the arguments, reasoning, thoughts, etc. Most audiences are both receptive and pliable.

THE SPEECH makes the speaker's case.

- ❖ The Toastmaster's introduction establishes credibility.
- ❖ The title frames the topic to be discussed.
- ❖ The Speaker's own introduction within the speech sets expectations or announces intentions.
- ❖ The main body of the speech provides evidence or supporting arguments.
- ❖ The closing usually summarizes or ties together the topic. and, ideally, capitalizes on the case that's been made.

THE RESULT is the audience's response—a desire to act, a decision to change or consider an opinion, an emotional connection. These results are the true measures of a speech's success.

Despite the speaker's having invested so much time and preparation in their speech, there's often a lack of follow through at the speech's end.

Speakers generate momentum; they build the case within their speech, only to shy away from pressing their conclusion forcefully. And it's their loss. What, if anything, happens as a result of an audience having heard the speech? Are hearts swayed? Are people moved to action? Most times the answer, sadly, is no. The desired result has not been achieved.

A sample speech

Consider the Toastmaster who wants to give a persuasive speech on the importance of exercise. First the speaker would research their topic and then outline their speech.

OUTLINE

TITLE:
Exercise Your Rights!

INTRODUCTION
Introduce topic and scope of speech: the importance of exercising as preventative medicine to increase life expectancy, improve quality of life.

TRENDS COMPROMISING OUR HEALTH
Technology is replacing our manual labor
Our lifestyle is more sedentary
Advent of fast food has added more calories to our diet

BENEFITS OF EXCERCISE
As little as 30 minutes a day of exercise reaps the following benefits:
- Strengthens cardio-vascular system— stave off heart attacks
- Strengthen immune system— helps ward off illness
- Provides mental stimulation
- Lower our cholesterol levels
- Relieve high blood pressure
- Reduce stress
- Aid in weight control
- Improves our memory

CLOSE:
"So get out there and exercise your rights."

A speech using this structure would likely be met with agreement by many, if not most, listeners. But it could be more persuasive, powerful and persuasive if the speaker chose to capitalize on the case made with a more compelling conclusion.

Where do we go from here?

Audiences listen politely to speakers as they state their case. At speech's end, audiences must form an opinion about the speech topic and content, if they haven't already. Some might agree, others disagree. Others still may be undecided or feel neutral about the topic, due to content, construction or delivery. Yet they look to the speaker for cues about where to go and what to do next. They ask, "Now what?" And so often speakers don't lead them to the answer they seek.

Take Your Listeners *One Step Beyond*

Powerful speakers know they can take license with audiences at the end of their speeches. Since speakers are leaders, they can lead their audience to more than just applause. How would you take the sample speech on exercise further? How would you mobilize your audience to action? How could you move them further with a more powerful closing?

Six ways to CLOSE this and other speeches with POWER

At the end of your speech:

1. Tell them what YOU will do.
   "When this speech is over I am going to walk around my local track for 40 minutes."

2. Issue a Call to Action.
   Challenge your listeners to do something:
   "I challenge you to calendar two hours for exercise before our meeting next week." (Hold up your calendar as a visual cue.)

3. Ask your audience to take an oath
   Raise your right hand and repeat after me:
   "I hereby promise to ..."

4. Lead them (you do it!):
   "Join me in a short stretching interlude: please stand and we'll do this exercise together: (describe excercise)"

5. Give them the tools to take the next step:
   "Here's a list of local gyms and health clubs to choose from, as well as exercise classes at the local adult school."

6. Put it in Writing!
   Invite your audience to write down their next action step, goals or plans as a result of your speech. Whether they turn it in to you or post it for themselves, you've built in some accountability for them.
   "Fill out this piece of paper with your action step. Write it on the top and bottom, date it, sign it and put a due date on it, and tear off the bottom and return to me. I will contact you on that date to confirm your accomplishment!"

It's Closing Time

The next time you listen to speeches in your Toastmasters club, see how far other speakers go in their closing. While not every speech is intended to be persuasive, inspirational or motivational, many are. In these cases, identify ways the speeches can close with power and lead their audiences to action. And the next time you give a persuasive speech, be more than just a speaker, be a leader too. Whether you're speaking in a contest or in your home club, close with power and extend your sphere of influence as a result.

Creative Strategies for Answering Table Topics

Let's face it, many of us are confident when we know what we're talking about. When the topic is one we're knowledgeable about, it's a snap. Ask an athlete about sports or a car buff about the new Mustang, and that person is home free. But what about the topic of particle physics or judicial restraint? Unless you're a scientist or student of jurisprudence, you're seemingly in trouble. But wait, don't panic. You may be better off than you realize.

Table Topics can be the most daunting part of each Toastmasters meeting, and it can also be the most fun. The key is to understand different ways you can answer topics when they're put to you. Plus, you already have many of the tools to succeed in this form of public speaking.

The Good, Bad & Ugly of Table Topics

Most participants in Table Topics have experienced both joy and pain. They've "nailed" topics successfully or floundered as they try to acquit themselves. Sometimes we're eloquent, other times embarrassed by our own feeble attempts to express ourselves cogently. We've all have the sensation of responding, returning to our seat, and only then recognizing "what we should have said!" That's natural.

Yet each topic answered is a success. My definition of success:

1. Answering the call
2. Staying within time limits
3. Giving a good faith effort to answer the question

My definition of failure:

1. Not even trying
2. Quitting in the middle
3. Saying "I don't know"

Excellent Table Topic responses, to me, are ones that are interesting, entertaining, timely, and/or thought provoking. I prefer responses that contain a catchy beginning, a well reasoned middle and end with a twist or some oomph.

Less-than-stellar Table Topic responses, in my opinion, are disjointed, meandering, unfocused, comprised of strings of non-sequiturs, or any response that just fizzles out.

Table Topics as Mini Speeches

True, you don't know the topic ahead of time, but in many other respects you should approach Table Topics question the same way as a prepared speech. Prepare for your next Table Topics by considering one or two of the following ideas:

❖ Preparing your Mind

❖ Did you read today's paper or listen to the news on TV or radio?

❖ Be topical. Know the issues of the day. (You'd be surprised how often the topics come from this area.)

What are today's issues?

- ▶ Wall Street collapse
- ▶ Hollywood scandal
- ▶ Horrific plane or car crash
- ▶ War or Strife

What have YOU been doing lately?
Did something interesting, strange or special happen to you (or a friend) recently? What's new with your kids, wife or husband? Go on vacation recently? Have a memorable meal? Read a good book or see a hot movie lately? All are topical for your response.

What's happening in your club? What happened to a fellow club member that others know about? Or don't know about?

Pay attention to the meeting! What did the speaker before you say? What else has been said already in your meeting? Is there an official theme for the day? Any unofficial themes emerging? Freudian slips, puns or malapropisms? Gauge the sentiment in the room. What's the mood?

Add to a theme or direction emerging in the meeting. Or perhaps contrast it. Be aware of what is happening in the situation. Anything your club members say or do is fair game.

Prepare your Body

One of the most common pitfalls for Table Topics respondants occurs before they've begun. They tense up. Their body becomes rigid, their breathing constricted, and thus, their mind becomes knotted.

Instead, stride up to the podium confidently. Shoulders back, standing up straight. Breathe deeply to bring oxygen into your system. I was taught to inhale in as if I was smelling a rose, then exhale as if I was blowing out a candle. (Deeper breathing will CALM you, but don't hyperventilate.)

Clear your throat as you walk up. Feel comfortable in whatever you're wearing. Wet your lips or lubricate mouth with a sip of water, coffee or juice. Beware of soda pop; you're liable to burp right in the middle of your topic!

And SMILE! This will relax you, the Table Topics master and even the audience. They will either struggle along with you or sail. Put everyone at ease. Remember, you're selling yourself, and the sales job begins before you've uttered your first words. When you feel confident you are confident.

Thoughts on Openings

The key to Table Topics: be decisive at the beginning! I advocate going with your first instinct. Whatever flashes through your mind initially is probably the kernel you'll want to build your response around (unless, of course, it's derogatory).

Don't over think! It's better to think out loud as you go than to try to over-analyze the topic before starting. You ought to be able to wing it for 90 seconds without articulating a policy statement! Some people become too cerebral with a topic. If you catch yourself in this mode, stop. You're probably over thinking.

Furthermore, you can leverage the topic through your inflection by questioning it, turning it into a statement, or otherwise providing a slant to the topic.

Remember:

1. You don't have to respond right away. Some people don't even turn toward the audience until they're ready to begin.

2. If the topic isn't clear, ask for it to be repeated to you.

3. If it doesn't click just yet, don't panic. You may want to repeat the topic out loud. Once you've uttered the words, they become yours. You've taken ownership. You've bought into it. This is important. Evaluate how it sounds when you say it. Is it believable? To you? To the audience? This will determine where you feel comfortable taking your topic.

Thoughts on Endings

End by feel. Like a comedian on The Tonight Show, you have a predetermined amount of time allotted. But a comic may end the same set on a different joke each night, depending on crowd reaction. You should do likewise. Gauge for yourself when to end your Table Topic. You don't always have to wrap up your speech with a nice bow. Leave 'em laughing, or pondering, in suspense, in doubt or even fuming.

But don't just peter out. Your ending should be decisive, emphatic and discernibly an ending.

You can also emulate gymnasts who use theatrics to let the audience know when their routine has concluded. When they "stick" their landing, they compose their body, stand erect, beam a giant smile at the audience and outstretch their arms in a show of confidence. Success is theirs!

Approaches to Table Topics

I've identified a number of strategies to employ when responding to table topics. These are sure-fire frameworks for presenting your thoughts in verbal form.

Bridging

Getting from what you don't know…to what you do know is the key in this technique. The sooner you build your bridge, the quicker you'll be on safe ground!

> **Topic:** Your car didn't start this morning. How would you trouble-shoot it?
>
> **Problem:** You don't have a mechanical bone in your body. You don't even pump your own gas. Also, you're a nurse.
>
> **Solution:** Figure a way to "bridge" from what you don't know (fixing cars) to what you do know (mending humans).

Topic: How would you chair a peace negotiation between a Hamas leader and the Prime Minister of Israel?

Problem: You don't follow foreign affairs, aren't in the least interested in politics, don't care about Mideast issues.

Solution: Bridge to a familiar situation—feuding family. Describe approaches you'd use with Uncle Harry and Aunt Bess. Seating arrangements, small praise, patience and humor.

Reframing

Suppose you're hit with a topic you just don't like or one that's not right for you. Don't despair—reframe it as one you'd like to respond to. Redefine it as you feel it should be, or at least the way you'd like it to be. Keep the structure, but alter the subject. Rephrase the question or even challenge it; explain why the question given is not the right question at all!

Topic: Who's better, tennis players Rafael Nadal or Roger Fedderer?

Problem: Who cares? You don't.

Solution: Find a pair you do feel is worth comparing. Perhaps it's players Serena vs. Venus Williams or Opera tenors Placido Domingo vs. Luciano Pavarotti or maybe even that classic debate between Butter and Margarine.

Dialogue

A.K.A. thinking out loud, dialogue involves asking rhetorical questions of your audience as you reason together. You're also probing for areas you know well enough to continue with, as well as areas that the audience will react to. Consider this technique a closely monitored stream of consciousness.

Quotes, Jokes and Sayings (use what you know)

Does the topic remind you of a quote? Or a joke? Or a saying? You can latch onto that to jump-start your response. Remember, you're buying time to think, brainstorming and drawing the audience in at the same time.

The Monodrama

Take the audience into your mind as you reason, out loud, the answer to the question. Tell us how you'd accomplish something or what you'd experience as something happens to you—from your travails as a tourist in an inhospitable country to preparing for your first blind date in years. (I derived a speech, then an hour-long workshop out of that ill-fated night!) Share your thoughts on the way to the altar or relive the most embarrassing moment from school days. Don't just recount it, take us there, immerse us in the experience and relive it with your entire body.

The Far Side

Take your topic to extremes. By exaggerating or embellishing, you heighten the seriousness or absurdity, whichever the case may be. This may involve asking a "What if…" or "Just suppose…" If you're telling a story, it will soon become a tall tale. If your topic has drama, you'll heighten it to melodrama. Absurdity is actually less threatening to an audience.

> **Topic:** Should we raise taxes?
>
> **Response:** Absolutely. Not only should we raise taxes, but—read my lips—just think of the benefits we'll achieve when we raise the tax rate **to 98%**.
>
> We'll have all the money we need for programs, defense, and government. We can bail out everybody!
>
> Then we can all buy stock in the IRS.
>
> We won't need banks and investment counselors.
>
> Nobody will have money to shop so there will be fewer TV commercials and billboards. Won't life be wonderful!

The Moderator (A.K.A. Point-Counterpoint)

Rather than take one side of an issue that you may or not be prepared to argue strenuously enough, take the middle road by representing both sides. Imagine yourself as Oprah, the impartial moderator, airing both sides and straddling the middle. We all know a couple of arguments for and against issues such as gun control, smoking in public or raising taxes.

This is a safe approach for a Toastmasters meeting and it provides great practice for outside encounters where being noncommittal is preferable. Use a few simple phrases to let the audience know where you're heading:

> On the one hand we all know…(45 seconds)
> But then again, consider the flip side (45 seconds)
> (Choose an ending) Take your pick, or do nothing.
> I'm for both, etc.

You Came From Outer Space

Step out of yourself to respond to a table topic. Be an extraterrestrial and put an alien spin on the topic. Instead of being Joe Blow from District 32, answer as if you're a stranger in a strange land. A corollary is pretending to be someone from another country.

> **Topic:** [provided by your Topics master]
>
> **Response:** I'm Mork from Planet Ork, what is this thing I'm observing?

Transcend Time

You needn't answer as yourself in January 2009. Assume the character and sensibilities of another person in time, real or fictional.

> Topic: Rosanne Arnold, love her or hate her?
>
> Response: I'm Roy Rogers and I just met a person I don't like…in my time we never heard of a woman who burped in public, or aired her dirty laundry in public. Why…

> Topic: your thoughts on family values?
>
> Response: I'm Moses and I better climb the mountain and bring back lots of revisions.

Consider this:

> Topic: Freeway traffic
>
> Response: Captain's Log: Stardate 5419…investigating planet comprised of millions of multi-colored rectangular projectiles traversing established corridors. When mating occurs, infrequently, others pass by slowly, some flashlights and motion can come to complete stops.

Compare & Contrast

This is an old favorite of authors, poets and even political candidates. It has built-in counterpoint. Take what you're given, and compare it to its opposite. What would your great grandfather say about this? It's giving voice to the devil's advocate.

> Topic: Should the government spend more money on education?
>
> Response: Instead of voicing one opinion, play with both sides of the argument.

Everyone Loves a Mystery

Build suspense into your response. Leave us in suspense. Leave us with a question or at least some doubt. Paint a picture but leave a few strokes unpainted. Or set us up to expect one picture before surprising us with another. Give us a twist. Shock us! Introduce speculation, a shadow of a doubt or an unknown element. You might even end on a question or in mid-sentence.

When All Else Fails…Say Nothing (at Length)

If you're absolutely 100% stumped, don't give in. Speak, but don't say anything. Use a string of openings, small talk, clichés or even gibberish. Remember, content is only part of the presentation. Body language, inflection, nuances and other embellishments all contribute to a successful topic response.

Repeat the question, repeatedly.

>**Topic:** To Be or Not to Be?
>
>**Response:** I thank you for asking me that profound question.
>To be or not to be. (pause)
>To BE or not to BE
>To be or NOT, to be. That is the question.
>Or is it?
>Is it or Is it Not.
>That is to Be…*determined.*

Topic: To Be or Not to Be, that is the question

Response: I'm glad you asked that question. For throughout time, that has been the question. I've read it in books, heard it on stage and wondered it myself. **To Be or Not to Be.** And whether or not you know the answer, or can explain it to others, it is a question you must ultimately answer for yourself. **To Be or Not to Be.** Some questions have a yes or no answer. Others are multiple choice. Still others are trick questions. If ever there were a $64 question this would be it. **To Be or Not to Be.** They say that is the question, but I say it is more of a dilemma, a conundrum, a riddle, a mystery of life, and a darn good Table Topic. But rather than let it work me up, I remain nonplused. After all, to worry about whether **To Be or Not to Be** is really **much ado about nothing!**

One contestant I know gave a Table Topic response entirely in *Chicken*: every utterance was a form of bawk, bawk, bawk... Unfortunately he was disqualified...for fowl language!

So good luck, have fun, and don't run any of the timekeeper's red lights!

Be a Creative Table TopicMaster

If variety is the spice of life, then creativity provides the flavor for Table Topics.

One way to induce creative responses to topics is to make the topics themselves creative. By setting a fun and festive tone as TopicMaster, you will find that, even for members who claim to be devoid of creativity, the spirit becomes contagious.

Here is a baker's dozen of ideas to stimulate creative participation in Table Topics when you're the TopicMaster.

Recipes for fun. As TopicMaster you're wearing a chef's cap or apron. You approach the front and spread out various ingredients and utensils, some familiar and others peculiar.

Challenge each person to pick some number of ingredients and a limited number of utensils and describe what they're preparing, how they'd prepare it, when and where they'd serve it and how it tastes. Is it a special remedy, a holiday recipe, an aphrodisiac or the way to rid the house of unwelcome company?

Newscast. Welcome to Toastmasters News. As TopicMaster you're the anchorperson, Rather B. Rich. Call on speakers as your correspondents to "report" on stories such as:

> The Tower of Babel (Babble!)
>
> An archeological find—the remains of Java man indicate he was wearing a Toastmaster pin.
>
> Esperanto (the international language) as the new standard in school

The language of love: discussing the rise and significance of a 1-900 Love Line

New class in School's Speech Department on Filibusters.

"**Psssst,** Secrets." you whisper as TopicMaster while leaning forward. Everybody has them, nobody shares them, normally. As Topics master, challenge each member to share a secret they've never shared before, or else describe one they already divulged and the consequences of their doing so. It's a chance to get personal with each other, share closely held aspects of each other and build closeness within the club.

JUMBLE. Spell the word TOASTMASTERS out on a flip chart posted for all to see. Now challenge each respondent to approach the sheet, create one word of 4 letters or more from the letters in TOASTMASTERS, and then speak on that word for 1-2 minutes. (Don't allow previous speakers' words to be used again.)

Start off by making a word of your own. Don't worry, there are over 30 words you can make from Toastmasters! A few examples include stream, start, roast, store, stem, tester, matter, storm, etc.

Provide bonus points for longest word or a word related to communication.

Fill in the Blank. Provide the speakers with the beginning of a phrase and let them finish it their way for 1-2 minutes. Examples:

"A funny thing happened on the way to the forum…"

"If Pigs could Fly…"

If I Had a Hammer…"

"Four Score and Seven Years Ago..."

"(S)he Who Laughs Last..."

The Press Conference. Encourage speakers to have fun with this topic. Your attention please! Our Press Conference will now begin. Each club member is called upon as an official of some organization to give a one-minute platform speech, then answer spontaneous questions from the press, your club's members, for next minute.

Know your members well enough to assign official titles appropriately: Commissioner of Baseball (to a sports fan), Attorney General (to a lawyer or police officer), Secretary of Defense (to someone serving in the Armed Forces), Executive Director for the National Organization of Women (to an ardent feminist), Surgeon General (to a doctor), Executive Director of the National Federation of Independent Businesses (for someone self-employed). That way, setting policy, even as a Table Topic, is a dream come true.

Ask each speaker to define their platform or agenda, then defend, clarify or elaborate upon it while answering follow-up questions.

Fable Topics. Challenge speakers to give a 21st century ending to a traditional fairy tale or fable.

Start it off with an example: Cinderella going to detox; Pinocchio having plastic surgery; Snow White issuing paternity tests for the dwarfs; Rapunzel charging a stranger with harassment.

Brushes with Fame. Andy Warhol posited that one day everyone would have 15 minutes of fame. Now it's your club members' turns.

Ask each person to describe their 15 minutes, if they've had it already. If not, ask how they'd like their fifteen minutes to be or what their claim to fame would be.

Timely Topics. Base topics on events that occur at that time of the year. For example, during mid-April ask taxing questions such as what one deduction would you allow? For April Fools Day tell lies (as Boastmasters). For Halloween, let the topic be Tall Tales. On Sadie Hawkins Day, the theme can be role reversals. On Veterans Day, celebrate freedoms.

The Postman Ringeth! Dressed as a postman with a satchel in tow, it's time for mail call. Fill your bag with a postcard from Tahiti, junk mail, a notification letter from the Publisher's Clearinghouse Sweepstakes, love letters in perfumed envelopes, funny or offbeat magazines, or a parcel with postage due. Have members reach into your mailbag, pick one of the goodies and respond to it for 1-2 minutes.

Your Virtual Coaches

Let the Internet Become Your Co-Pilot

A good Toastmaster has many tools at her or his disposal. Once upon a time, the local library supported members as they researched topics, looked up word origins in the dictionary and otherwise sought reference materials.

Today, the World Wide Web brings you more information faster and from the farthest reaches of the globe. Each week I find facts, figures and frivolity I can apply to my weekly role in my club. What an indispensable tool for Toastmaster success!

WordMaster

When I'm our club's WordMaster, choices abound. First I'll check my e-mail in-box. Like 520,000 other people in 201 countries, I subscribe to the free "A Word a Day" service of www.Wordsmith.org. Recently, the word of the day was *armamentarium*. (It means the collection of equipment and techniques available to one in a particular field.) Hmmm, I won't win any friends with this one! But I wonder if our Sergeant-at-arms knows the word?

Next I check the free Words of the Month posted by District 56 Toastmaster VJ Singal at www.verbalenergy.com. VJ authored the book *The Articulate Professional* and has helped thousands build their vocabulary through his site. His words have added polish and professionalism to my speeches and day-to-day dialogue. Ever since meeting VJ at a Toastmasters International Convention, my vocabulary, and that of my club's, has expanded exponentially!

Opening Thought

A new member of our club has been given her first assignment...Opening Thought. She's at a loss to find a quote to match next week's meeting theme. She e-mails me, her newly assigned mentor, for help. After a chat on the phone, I send her one of many links to quotation pages: www.startingpage.com/html/quotations.html#bestlistings. If it's worth quoting, it's here or linked from here. Of course I encourage her by suggesting that some day she'll say something so profound she will be quoted by others. She responds with a combination of appreciation and bemusement. Nevertheless, the idea has been planted!

Once, I was asked the night before a meeting to provide the week's Opening Thought. I wanted to share something inspirational. A double click later I had my choice of many on www.realage.com! The site offers uplifting health-related tips that keep me as centered, balanced and aligned as my car. Also check out www.motivational-inspirational-corner.com/motivational inspirational quotes.html. Depending on the theme of the day, or my mood, I'll use this site's search engine to find an appropriate quote by either topic or source.

Toastmaster of the Day

Over the years a variety of sites have helped me as Toastmaster. Some I visit on a regular basis for ideas and tips to apply in meetings.

The 3M Meeting Network at www.3m.com/meetingnetwork/ has many meeting resources to help Toastmasters plan, implement and evaluate meetings, as does their e-zine (www.3m.com/meetingnetwork/form_newsletter.html).

To answer questions about parliamentary procedure, I often surf Robert's Rules of Order (www.robertsrules.com) before planning and conducting meetings. I especially like the site's question and answer forum where I can post questions, view past discussions and more.

To find out what happened on a given day in history, I visit www.scopesys.com/cgi/today2.cgi. As Toastmaster of the Day, I can share the names of famous people who were born or died on that day and historic events that occurred. For example, on January 21, I could state that on the same date in 1789, the first American novel, W.H. Brown's "The Power of Sympathy," was published. Opera tenor Placido Domingo was born in Madrid, Spain in 1941, and in 1950 author George Orwell [born Eric Arthur Blair] died from tuberculosis in London. Who knew!

By the way, did you know every day's a holiday somewhere in the world? Visit groups.yahoo.com/group/multicultural-holidays/ for information on today's holiday!

Writing and Giving a Speech

The Internet is full of sites that archive great speeches, whether by statesmen and stateswomen, scientists or artists and poets of any era. There are political speeches, famous commencement addresses and other oratory that have withstood the test of time. Such texts and transcriptions are often revealing and inspiring at the same time.

When it's time to pick a speech topic, I am often inspired by subjects featured in television programs aired on the Public Broadcasting System (PBS) in the United States. Their site, www.pbs.org/, lets me dig deeper on any topic covered by a PBS program.

For more extensive research, try the United States Library of Congress site, which is full of books in print www.loc.gov. To learn anything related to any branch of the US Government, go to www.fedworld.gov/firstgov.html.

Speech delivery tips are also plentiful on the World Wide Web. Toastmasters own site, (www.toastmasters.org), has tips on giving speeches plus articles, tips and guides to speechmaking from Districts around the world. I've even been known to upload to a few such sites to share my own wisdom. I hope you do, too.

SpeakerNet News You Can Use

My secret speaker weapon comes from www.SpeakerNetNews.com. *SpeakerNet News* is a weekly compilation of speaker tips from over 5,000 professional speakers, trainers, consultants, authors and vendors from around the world. It's free, it's e-mailed to me each Friday, and it's chock full of fascinating tips to help me be more impactful as a speaker. There are platform and performance tips, recommendations on audio-visual equipment and so much more.

Just last week alone, I picked up a tip on how to be a better emcee, learned some insider secrets for designing and delivering PowerPoint presentations, and even read about a website (www.t-mail.com/cgi-bin/tsail) that will translate other sites into the language of your choice! I'll no longer be Lost in Translation.

The best part of *SpeakerNet News* is that you can pose questions of its 5,000 communicators and get a variety of responses to your queries. If you want to research a certain audience, a region or a culture, ask *SpeakerNet News*. If you want suggestions on powerful speech opening, closings or use of props, ask *SpeakerNet News*. It's a wonderful virtual community full of sharing and support that you can easily tap into.

Closing Thought

There are so many sites to help you choose a closing thought. Some days I prefer Shakespeare: www.allshakespeare.com/quotes. Other weeks I opt for the poetry of Rumi: www.allspirit.co.uk/rumi.html. On occasion I prefer funny or quizzical quotes and ruminations such as those found on www.comedy-zone.net/guide/quotes.htm or funny things other people, including kids, have said: www.rinkworks.com/said/.

Joke Master

Several free services that e-mail me a joke a day include www.joke-a-day.com and www.ajokeaday.com. The two challenges I find in delivering humor in Toastmasters are picking the right joke and telling it from memory. These sites give me ample content to choose from. Jokes are clean, short and plentiful, so the odds of finding the right joke for my club mates, meeting theme and tone are high.

I've bookmarked the late John Cantu's site www.humormall.com and revisit it often. John remains a humor helper to Toastmasters worldwide through his rich humor-laden website.

On a monthly basis I receive the warm and gentle humor of Karyn Buxman's *LyteBytes*, www.humorx.com. There's also the enjoyable *HumorPower* e-zine from professional humorist and Toastmaster John Kinde's site www.HumorPower.com. I visit www.familyjokeaday.com and many topical joke sites and services. Depending on the type of humor you prefer, you may surf the web for riddle sites, spoonerisms, knock-knock jokes, and more.

Grammarian

I've found various sites over the years that help me be a better grammarian. Wordsmith Barbara McNichols's site www.barbaramcnichol.com alerts me to *word trippers*, teaching me which homonym is the right word to use in every situation. Her e-zine brings tips like these to me regularly.

One site that offers a portal to over a hundred relevant links comes through Toastmaster-favorite Dr. Richard Lederer pw1.netcom.com/~rlederer/rllink.htm. Sites linking to this page address grammar and usage, etymology, linguistics, puns, oxymorons and much more. For idioms of speech heard in meetings, I use and refer others to www.phrases.org.uk/meanings/. This site explains turns of phrase and colloquialisms not commonly known by all members.

Speaking Outside of Toastmasters

When I am asked to give a speech outside of Toastmasters, I use the Internet to research the group, audience or location. When I speak at a new club demonstration meeting for a local company, I use www.hoovers.com to learn more about them and recent events. I'll also look at related newsgroups found through search engine Google's group category www.google.com/grphp?hl=en&tab=wg&ie=UTF-8 to learn more about companies or organizations. You can too!

After Meetings

Often I hear figures of speech during meetings that I am unfamiliar with. Various sites offer etymological information on turns of phrase, idioms of speech and vernacular expressions one hears in meetings. These sites allow me to learn outside Toastmasters meetings. I've been known to send out a postscript to our meeting with any follow-up information, clarifications or elucidations on topics addressed in our meeting. It's a form of "lagniappe" I believe in—giving Toastmasters "a little something extra" to enhance the meeting experience.

When I want further dialogue on a topic broached at a club meeting, I use Google's talk search for appropriate online discussion forums to interact with: groups.google.com/groups?group=talk&hl=en.

Ideas for your Club

I've become a big fan of the newsgroup alt.toastmasters.org. It's a virtual group worth subscribing to. As a member of this free cyber-community you can pose questions of Toastmasters worldwide and learn from thousands of others who've traveled the same path. Check this listserv out!

Many clubs, Districts and regions have their own virtual groups to share information, opinions and resources. Tap into these virtual Toastmaster communities for local and regional news and nuggets.

Since 1924 Toastmasters has been making effective oral communication a worldwide reality. Now the World Wide Web helps us all connect to each other. Let the Internet be your virtual coach as you matriculate within Toastmasters. Happy clicking!

How To Learn Customer Service as a Club Officer

A Seven-Point Program for Mastering Customer Service

Did you know that Toastmasters provides a 7-point program for mastering customer service? It takes less time than a 4-year degree and can be pursued in your home club.

True, it's not publicized in any Toastmaster documentation, but I am a graduate of this program. Allow me to explain. Over 42 months, I served in all seven club leadership positions. In the process, I became an expert in customer service! Here's how.

Sergeant Salutes Guests

I initially became my club's sergeant-at-arms. I was responsible for making guests feel welcome. I arrived early before each meeting, set up the room and made sure our guest register book and literature were set out in anticipation of guests. I made sure our sign was affixed outside the door, and I wore my badge to identify myself for our new customers—the guests visiting for the first time.

Then, as timid and tentative visitors arrived, I made them feel welcome with a smile, an outstretched hand and a genuine interest in them. Toastmasters taught me to treat guests like visiting royalty. I anticipated their needs for comfort, safety and information, and provided each. I told them how happy we were they joined us, how they were under no pressure to speak, and then introduced them to an experienced member to sit by their side during the meeting to answer any questions they had.

My sergeant-at-arms role also demonstrated the importance of my duties as they related to the rest of the club. Without supplies in place, there would be no gavel to bang or lectern to speak from. It helped me think in terms of others, both the needs of the members and the scary and intimidating feelings I had arriving as a first time visitor to the club.

Secretary: Members' Pipeline to World Headquarters (WHQ)

Next I became my club's Secretary. In this role I helped document members' transactions with the club, District and WHQ. I used my written communication skills to fix problems and correct errant information. I created a paper trail for my customers—our club members—who joined, transferred or rejoined after a hiatus. I assisted other officers in their paperwork by insuring officer lists were accurate and submitted properly, among other tasks. Minutes I prepared during officer's meetings became the record of our decisions on behalf of our members.

In this role I was responsible for clear communication with a service orientation to make sure members received value from their membership. At the same time, I helped strengthen our Area, Division and District by keeping our club in compliance.

VP-Membership: Paying Attention to Retention

Six months later, when I served as VP Membership, I really honed my listening skills, a key aspect of effective customer service. I began to understand my club members' goals and their needs and what I could do to help address them. By listening to what members said, I came to understand how they thought, what motivated them and how we could help them succeed. Their success was my success.

I became an expert at retention as I worked to keep each member engaged and happy as a customer of the club. I also began to pay attention to problems that periodically arose in meetings or among membership and applied myself to solve these problems to the satisfaction of our members. These moments of truth became opportunities for me to champion their needs and help the club serve each member. By caring for each member, I was selflessly serving his or her needs.

VP-PR: Promoting Solutions to Others' Problems

Soon thereafter, I was elected to be my club's Public Relations VP. I was now charged with attracting new members. I began to think again in terms of new customers—non-members who had needs I could fill. They had fears, and I had remedies. They had desires, and I had outcomes. Or as past International Director Joe McBride puts it, "They had itches I could scratch."

I promoted the Toastmasters programs with pride as I observed a world of potential new customers that had yet to experience the benefits I was receiving as a member. Solving peoples' problems, giving them confidence, new skills, new resources and opening their world were all forms of customer service, and I reveled in being the solution to their problems.

Treasurer: Investing in the Success of Others

When elected Treasurer, I began to safeguard our members' investment in the club. Through fiscal responsibility, I ensured our club was able to purchase supplies to educate, recognize and support each member.

By insuring our dues were collected and submitted on time, I served our club's contestants insuring they and our club remained in good standing so they could experience the joys, growth and glory of competing. I felt like an unsung hero as I helped our club manage its finances well enough to hold an open house, host a contest and underwrite a Youth Leadership Program for a local middle school. My reports during business meetings reinforced the value members received by detailing of the benefits when I described how our club dues were spent helping them and others experience success.

VP, Education: The Answer is "Know"

As I began my term as the club's VP, education I was feeling like an upper classman. I used my past experience as a speaker and an officer to help my fellow members. As EVP, I was responsible for serving the educational needs of each member. Yet each had different needs. I came to understand the underpinnings of Customer Relationship Management and treated each member the way they wanted to be treated. I made sure to know how to help each member.

Some aspired to complete their CC by June 30 and had a few speeches yet to deliver. I could help them succeed through my scheduling. Other members were trying to complete their AL and CL and I could help each with their ambitions. A Toastmaster from South Africa was visiting the San Francisco Bay Area in a month and hoped to give a speech while visiting our club. I arranged a theme meeting coinciding with this speaker's topic, and we built a program around his visit.

As an experienced officer I could provide added value to my members through my familiarity with Toastmasters' various educational materials. I could identify resources such as advanced manuals to assist them, and point them toward District roles and opportunities where they could flex their newfound communication and leadership muscles. I could help them be happy customers, achieving their goals and all the while helping our club pursue its critical success factors of CCs, CLs, ACs, ALs, retention and growth.

President: Leading a Customer Relationship Management (CRM) Firm

It was when I was elected president that I realized I was actually leading a service organization. Our officers were entrusted with running an organization to meet the diverse needs of our membership. Staging quality meetings, helping our members achieve their goals and providing a supportive team to advance these aims was my responsibility.

I empowered each officer to advocate for our new and continuing members. I communicated dutifully with my Area Governor and District Officers to keep apprised of programs, trainings and special events. And like a good manager I made sure my officers received training and support so they could support club members in turn.

Through serving the seven officers roles at the club level I learned the core values of customer service:

- ❖ Treat others the way they want to be treated
- ❖ Listen intently
- ❖ Focus on quality
- ❖ Think in terms of your customers
- ❖ Communicate clearly in word and writing
- ❖ Advocate for customers to help them succeed

Yes, in my own way I now feel I have a degree in customer service. It's as if I have my CC, my CL and now my CRM too. And just the other day, a District Officer asked me if I was ready to assume a new District role. Ah, graduate school beckons at the Toastmasters Institute of Customer Service.

II. MOTIVATION

During your tenure in Toastmasters, you may experience doubts that you will achieve your speaking or leadership goals. You may question yourself or your commitment to the program or wonder whether you should accept some of the challenges that come your way.

This section fortifies you with incentives to work Toastmasters' curricula extensively. You will learn how confidence is derived from each new experience and even experiences you repeat. Best yet, this section will give you confidence and motivation in other areas of your life as well!

Good, Better...BEST!

Turning Milestones into Stepping Stones

Milestone: *An important event or turning point in one's history or career.*

Stepping Stone: *An advantageous position for advancement towards some goal; something that assists an ambition.*

Great marathon runners got their start the same way we all did. As infants, they crawled before they walked. They rose, teetered and fell, then rose again and steadied themselves on a nearby object. Once they could stand in place, the view changed, as did their perspective. Then, a new goal was established...standing without props. Once this was achieved, they sought to walk. They started to ambulate. They fell. They struggled back to their feet and tried again. They had the confidence and hunger to set new goals...and thus, they finally walked. Then they realized they could see more if they picked up the pace. They set a new goal, and they began to run. Over time, progress became a question of whether they were going to be held back by others' limits or test their own limits of endurance and stamina. Finally, they ran marathons.

Dream...goal...try...fail...retry...milestone...new goal... failure...retry...success...

And so it goes. Seemingly unreachable milestones are achieved and then become stepping stones to further achievements. Whatever your goals, the formula can work for you as well.

Step-Aerobics!

It all starts with a dream. You dare to imagine doing something, going someplace, becoming someone and making a difference. Without the aspiration, nothing can happen. Yet how far do you get? Do you allow setbacks to slow or stop you? Do you lose confidence? Lose momentum? Lose faith? Many do.

Marathon runners know that theirs is a long race broken into many little races. Marathoners also know that sooner or later they will hit "the wall." Their ability to continue on is the key to their success. The wall is something to be overcome. It is not a stopping point, but simply another milestone along the way. They step over the wall and use it as a stepping stone to ultimate success.

Step One: Setting Goals

The best way to achieve milestones is to have them in your sights from the beginning. We can do this through setting goals.

As children, our parents and teachers set goals for us. Since our youth, we've set goals for ourselves, too. In Toastmasters we set goals upon joining. Why did you join? Was it to acquire a new skill? To overcome an old phobia? Was it a personal challenge? Did your boss send you? Whatever the reason for joining, you arrived with at least one goal. Perhaps you set new ones once you filled out your member profile, met with a mentor and learned about the many programs Toastmasters offered.

Your club's Educational Vice President (EVP) may also have set goals for you, in concert with your own goals. EVPs know the curricula and know how to help you turn your aspirations into achievements. Common goals could include the ability to make a speech at work, to be perceived as a strong communicator in the office, to gain confidence meeting and conversing with strangers at social gatherings or other goals as well.

Goals help us become focused and give us purpose. Each goal we set can be pursued. Once achieved, the goal becomes a milestone and then a stepping stone to further accomplishment.

Step Two: Getting Started

According to the great American novelist Mark Twain, "Twenty years from now you will be more disappointed by the things that you didn't do than by the ones you did do. So throw off the bowlines. Sail away from the safe harbor. Catch the trade winds in your sails. Explore. Dream. Discover." We've heard so often that a journey of a thousand miles begins with a single step. Once we make that initial step, we're on our way, however far we must go.

When you think about it, attending your first meeting is a milestone. You might scoff at the notion that just showing up at a meeting is a milestone. Yet for many people, fear overrides their ability to do even the simplest tasks. Lack of confidence will keep them from socializing, exploring new environs and meeting new people. That's why Toastmasters offers visitors such a gracious welcome. Club members know it will open the door to visitors' future success.

Speaking for the first time from the lectern is another milestone. When new members join a club, they are shepherded in and carefully nurtured. They often are given a simpler assignment for their first role so they can experience success, get their legs under them and not taste defeat in their initial time out. Wasn't that your experience?

Step Three: Gaining Momentum

Every new year we announce our new resolutions with excitement. Within the month, many of them have fallen by the wayside. Our intentions were good, yet our resolve was not firm.

When we pursue a milestone, we'll make discernible progress on some days, and on other days we won't. Sometimes the milestones require weeks, months or even years of effort to realize. For club officers, it's the pursuit of distinguished club status; for governors, it's a Distinguished Area, Division or District. For some speakers, the status of Accredited Speaker is your ultimate goal. None of these can be achieved overnight. The key, then, is maintaining resolve. We must keep our goals in sight at all times and endeavor to make progress every day, every week and every month. An object in motion will stay in motion. An object at rest will remain so. So…get moving! Inertia is what it's all about.

Step Four: Persevering

But how do we keep the momentum going? How do we persevere? The secret comes from maintaining focus.

In our clubs we look to fellow members to help keep us focused. We make contracts with our club's EVP to pursue and achieve certain goals by the end of term or end of year. At work and at home, we often write our goals down and then post them in visible places as a constant reminder of the milestones we're pursuing. For some, "going public" is a way of leveraging a bit of friendly peer pressure from our supporters to help us maintain focus. No doubt, the recognition and support we receive along the way also helps us persevere. And as we near our milestone, a new form of motivation occurs as we see, sense and smell the finish line.

Step Five: Succeeding

With the finish line in sight, we plan our last triumphant steps. Sometimes we sprint for the finish line, and dash we do to cross the line of our self-defined goals and achieve our milestone. And then what? We take our bows, triumphantly accept the congratulations of others and graciously bask in the recognition given by others.

And yet, this success is not the final chapter at all. Success is just another weigh station. The great college basketball coach John Wooden put it well: "If you go as far as you can see, you will then see enough to go even farther."

Step Six: Gaining a New Perspective

As we survey the new heights we've attained, the view is discernibly different. Suddenly we see new mountaintops, new peaks and new possibilities. With our newfound confidence, what once seemed unattainable now is a fait accomplit. We did it. And now new challenges await. Our once high milestone is now firmly underfoot. We use it as a perch to see even higher or as a stepping stone to further greatness.

With our CC achieved, we set out to master new forms of communication on our way to our AC. Having served one role in the club, we volunteer for new and often greater responsibilities. The greater the challenge, the more satisfying the accomplishment. The greater the milestone, the more powerful a stepping stone it becomes to ultimate success.

Runners...On Your Marks

What goals have you set for yourself? What milestones are you pursuing? Have you gone public with your aspirations?

Poet Thomas Carlyle said it best: "The block of granite which was an obstacle in the path of the weak becomes a stepping stone in the path of the strong."

Step forth boldly!

Greater Things to Come:
Projecting Potential

> *The greatest good you can do for another*
> *is not just to share your riches,*
> *but to reveal to them their own.*
> — Benjamin Disraeli

Professional Speaker Jim Cathcart can look at an acorn and see a future oak tree. After seventeen years in Toastmasters, I can see similar potential in new members. Just as others saw my diamond in the rough, I now relish the opportunities to stoke the flames of newcomers and encourage them to greater pursuits. You can too!

Toastmasters should look not at the present limitations of members and guests but rather their potential for future greatness. We should also look at what we can do to help them realize their vast potential. The fact that someone saw beyond my ums and ahs, my rough edges and lack of polish, and then cared enough to invest time and training in me, has helped me become the communicator and leader that I am today. Even now, I'm a masterpiece in progress. Aren't you, too?

The greatness of Hockey Hall of Famer Wayne Gretzky was in his ability to skate not to where the puck was, but where it would soon be. We as experienced Toastmaster mentors and leaders must look at our members' existing talents as building blocks to future greatness. We must see their potential and envision where they're going. Especially since they cannot always see it themselves.

Whether through slow methodical progress or leaps and bounds, members are nevertheless on the road to self-improvement. Our ability to see beyond their present limitations, their perceived shortcomings or their lack of experience and confidence in a given area, may be just the springboard they need to realize new successes and new milestones.

Milestones as Stepping Stones

Remember your first Table Topic? Your Ice Breaker? The first time you were the day's Toastmaster? You may have doubted your ability to achieve each of these milestones. Yet, upon reaching that step, suddenly new goals emerged. The newfound confidence derived through achieving each milestone helped turn it into a stepping stone to further greatness.

As we mentor and coach newer members in our clubs, we can help them experience the thrill inherent in achieving each of these key milestones. Our experienced eyes can also envision what might be next for nascent members who aren't yet familiar with the various programs and opportunities available within Toastmasters.

Accentuating the Positive

Our speech evaluation training teaches us to look beyond what a speaker needs to improve and to, initially, focus on what he or she already does well. By identifying what core strengths they possess, we can help them build on their solid foundation.

This doesn't just apply to speakers giving their Ice Breakers.

By accentuating the positive in our new members, we reaffirm their competency and help them build confidence as they grow. When a member leads an effective meeting, competes admirably in a contest, or effectively recruits others to your club, each portends greater things to come. We should validate evident strengths as a way of nurturing and also encouraging potential yet to be tapped.

The Eyes Have It

What do you see when a new member joins your club? Look for sparks of creativity, trace elements of confidence and evidence of leadership potential to nurture. Look closely; it may be just beneath the surface. The key is to look for it. Then, it's easier to find.

I've met a new member who, though shy and quiet by nature, had a strong and confident voice; a foreign-born speaker struggling with English whose wonderful sense of humor emerged within a few weeks; another new member with such an air of authority that credibility oozed from her, even in her first tentative speeches. In each case, the evidence I saw was just the tip of the talent iceberg. Each of these people have come into their own, in part through the support of experienced members who recognized sparks of brilliance and nurtured them. Once the members saw their own talents, they could cultivate them for everyone's benefit.

Translating Potential into Reality

The fun really begins when the potential is realized. Suddenly new horizons appear when a member masters core competencies.

Thus we emphasize achieving one's Competent Toastmaster status. The CC forms the cornerstone for future communication success. Similarly, when members successfully serve as officers at the club level, their taste for leadership whets their appetite for more nourishing assignments. Many a District leader got his or her start as a club officer. I could never have served my District as its governor if my club mates hadn't supported me during my infancy as a green and tentative club president.

Today Cindy Ventrice, AC-B, is a professional speaker and author of *Make Their Day—Employee Recognition That Works* (www.maketheirday.com). Long before she was a professional speaker and author, her potential was recognized and nurtured by seasoned Toastmasters. Cindy said, "I know that many of the evaluations and notes that I have received over the years helped me to see that I had potential as a public speaker. If not for the members of Santa Cruz, CA's Downtown Toastmasters (#1803-4) I wouldn't have had the courage to become a professional speaker!"

You have the power to launch professional speakers, politicians, religious leaders, astronauts and more by nurturing others' potential. Step into your power by helping others translate their potential into potency! You'll take special pride in knowing you helped springboard a fellow member from tentative to talkative, from raw to ready, from meek to mellifluous. And in the process of nourishing others' potential you'll be extending your sphere of influence as a Toastmaster leader.

Finding Confidence:
Toastmasters Can Take You There!

> *"Men die of fright and live of confidence."*
> —Thoreau

I heard of a place called Confidence. I wanted to find it.

Others had been there, and it showed. Yet I hadn't found Confidence yet for myself.

I set out only knowing its general direction. Mine was to be an uphill journey. I drove and drove with nary a clue. At first, the road was long and flat with many cars going this way and that. Then it began to rise as I entered the foothills. The altitude reached 1,000 feet. The road began to twist and turn. Soon a sign said I'd reached 2,000 feet. The air was getting thinner. There were far fewer cars. I became short of breath. I passed the 3,000 foot sign. My pace slowed. Yet I pressed on. I wanted to find Confidence. I needed to find Confidence.

I was getting tired. It was getting late. I wondered if I'd ever find it. I thought my plan had been sound. I knew I was heading in the right direction. But discouragement began to overtake me. I reached 4,000 feet. And then I saw a sign. But, it wasn't the sign I was expecting. This sign said I was approaching... Turnback Creek!

Now the thoughts of quitting that I'd been ignoring hit me with the force of a grizzly bear. How elusive Confidence seemed at this moment. Should I turn back? Was my effort futile? Was I hopelessly lost? Would I ever find Confidence? Indeed this was my moment of truth!

What would it mean if I quit now? Was my effort in vain? What if I was actually close to my goal? Just how important was it for me to find Confidence? Could I look others in the eye if I saw a quitter when I looked in the mirror? It was decision time.

I wavered for what seemed like an hour. Although it was probably only five to seven minutes, plus or minus thirty seconds. I was giving a speech to myself. Could I convince my audience of one that I should persevere?

I remember having similar doubts when I first joined Toastmasters. After visiting the first time, I pondered not coming back. After my first Table Topic—57 seconds of terror—I wanted to hide under the table and never resurface. And after my Ice-Breaker I questioned whether I'd ever overcome my fear of public speaking. It took three weeks for me to return to my second meeting. Yet in each case, I did continue on my journey. However daunting, I persisted in my quest to find Confidence as a communicator.

And so I decided with my own Confidence that I would press on. I would stick to it! Now I had renewed vigor, a stronger resolve, a clear vision of my journey and an inner Confidence that my objective would be met. I still didn't know when or how, but I knew I would find this elusive Confidence.

It's true. It is darkest just before the dawn. And wouldn't you know it, just a few miles past Turnback Creek, I literally found Confidence!

The sign welcomed me: now entering Confidence, California. Altitude: 4,200 feet. I know I felt sky high. I found it!

I finally found Confidence. It was here all along.

I learned that day that you don't just stumble onto Confidence. You don't just reach Confidence. You experience it!

Craig finds Confidence, northeast of Yosemite in the Sierra mountain range of Northern California.

What a feeling to find what you set out to find. How rewarding to know that one's toil is ultimately rewarded. How fulfilling to finally grasp the elusive.

And having now experienced Confidence, I knew I could help others get there too.

The sign said "Population: 50." I was perplexed. Surely there were more than 50 people who had found Confidence. The locals in the Confidence Café explained that once people found Confidence, they could go anywhere, do anything and be whoever they wanted to be. Many former residents had left to spread the spirit of Confidence with others worldwide. And one of the ways they were doing so was through Toastmasters.

Fellow Toastmasters, Confidence beckons. She awaits you. Embrace her and all things are possible. Let Toastmasters be your guide to finding Confidence.

Take Two!
Value Derived from Serving A Second Time

We live in a world where people are quick to proclaim, "Been there, done that." Yet in my experience, it's often the second time I go somewhere or do something that I receive the full benefit of the experience. This has definitely been true in Toastmasters.

We are constantly learning, both within and outside of our club experiences. Sometimes we aren't even aware of how much we've grown until we find ourselves in a similar situation and realize we have new skills and qualities to offer.

For instance, the first time I served as a club President, it took me four months to even feel comfortable in the role. It was only several years later, when I became President of a specialty club, that I really came to appreciate what I could do in that role to lead our club to success.

As an Area Governor, it was all I could do to survive my first contest in the fall. Yet when it was time to plan the spring contest, I was filled with confidence, experience and a better understanding of what was expected and what possibilities existed.

I remember the first time I served as a meeting's Timekeeper. I was so proud of the precision with which I timed each speech, table topic and evaluation. Yet it was later, when I served as Timekeeper a second time, that I began to uncover other ways I could add value in that role: helping us start our meeting on time by giving a 30-second visual warning to our members, timing officer reports and giving flashes of yellow when unscripted portions of our meeting threatened to disrupt our day's timetable. I realized I could assist our President and Toastmaster of the day in driving the meeting from the back of the room, just as a hook and ladder fire truck has a driver leading from the front and another one steering from the rear. Together they deftly navigate the terrain. As Timekeeper, I could provide the same direction and leadership throughout the meeting from the back of the room.

The first time I played the role of Grammarian in our club, I diligently counted speakers' "ums and "ahs" and the occasional "and um." I then gave my report of peoples' shortcomings in this area. I noticed I wasn't the most popular member that day as I issued my news.

When next asked to fill the role, I initially demurred. Oh, I've done that before. Can't someone else do it? Then a past president told me how much she enjoyed the role. She liked to catch people doing things right, using appropriate words and employing nice turns of phrase. Suddenly, my eyes opened to the possibilities. Now I relish the role of Grammarian. I credit speakers who use alliteration and double entendres or who draw nice analogies. I bring my dictionary to the meeting and define words speakers use that may be new to some members. I still count filler words, but I do so much more. Only the second time around was I able to look beyond and stretch the envelope of my role as initially defined.

The same approach works for Toastmasters materials. I've completed what is now known as the *Competent Communication* manual not once, not twice, but three times since joining

Toastmasters in 1992. Each time I open it, I find ways of building on my current experience to get that much more out of each assignment.

Just as people will reread the Bible, textbooks and classic novels, I reread and rework Toastmasters programs I've completed previously. Each time I get something new. If that's not your experience, read a little deeper!

Albert Einstein said, "The important thing is never to stop questioning." Ask yourself how you can improve the quality of your club, meeting and District each time you serve.

Whether it is a Club or District office you are asked to serve a second time, or a role you've already played before in a meeting or special event, I challenge you to approach it with new eyes, new curiosity and newfound enthusiasm. The rewards will seem twice as sweet!

PDG Michelle Gilstrap with Craig during his keynote at Region II's Conference.

III. HUMOR

Humor is the elixir of life! It's the shortest distance between two strangers, it fulfills many of our own physical and psychological needs, and it's otherwise good for mind, body and soul.

Best yet, as Dr. Ralph C. Smedley, the founder of Toastmasters International, recognized eighty-odd years ago, we learn best during times of enjoyment. And that's why learning and laughter pair so well in Toastmasters. In both prose and poetry, this section celebrates the humor that occurs in meetings, in speeches and in our society at large. You will be entertained and educated. Remember: laugh, and the world laughs with you!

Good, Better...BEST!

Speakers Say the Darndest Things!

Amusing Things Overheard on the Platform from Toastmasters and Professional Speakers

With all due respect to Art Linkletter, speakers say the darndest things! And Toastmasters, fret not. Even professional speakers succumb to misstatements, missteps and foot-in-mouth disease from the platform. Perhaps that's not surprising given the amount of time we're on stage and the pressure we're under to perform.

The combination of pressure, excitement and nerves has been known to result in some amusing faux pas and malapropisms. Surprisingly, our audiences appreciate the comic relief provided by these misstatements. At times, our mistakes turn out to be the part of our performance they remember most.

Despite our preparation and rehearsal, sometimes words and phrases just don't come out the way we expect them to. Consider the Toastmaster working from the Communicating on Television manual. He was discussing handguns, firebombs and arson. His presentation was serious and his passion evident. Then, he asked the audience to consider "the danger inherent in radicals using *Molokai* cocktails" to inflict damage on property. The audience wondered if the meeting planner had hired the guy Hawaii 5 0 style—you know, "Book-em, Dan-o?"

Another time, a professional speaker being interviewed on radio was extolling the virtues of daily exercise. The host asked her if exercise really worked year-round. "Absolutely," she replied. "It works 375 days a year!" The silence that followed seemed an eternity. The host finally asked, "Did you say three hundred *seventy* five days a year?" To the speaker's credit, she regrouped and added, "Did I say that? That's an indication of *how much* I believe in it!" They say stretching is good for you, even in conversation!

This same speaker experienced a similar situation in a television interview. She knew what she wanted to say, but in the excitement of the moment, the words didn't flow in the right order. In the span of one five-minute segment, she described job opportunities for recent college graduates as "level entry" and referred to a major task as a "burst of beaden." She kept viewers engaged as they tried to figure out what she meant to say and hung on every word to hear what else she might jumble. Don't underestimate the heightened attention engendered by these misstatements.

Humorist and Certified Speaking Professional June Cline shared a case of unintended humor that came about by bungling a standard statement she uses at the start of her presentations. In a completely straight face, at the outset of one of her trainings, she asked attendees to "turn their vibrators on page." It's not clear whether her misstatement turned her audience off…or on! What is known is that the ensuing laughter did more to facilitate an effective training than any planned or contrived technique she could have employed.

We all know the value of provocative titles and dramatic openings to capture the attention of our audiences. Speaker beware, however, as you may be laying a trap for yourself or your introducer. Roseann Sullivan, a past president of the National Speakers Association's Northern California chapter, periodically delivers a workshop on marketing entitled "How to Hook a

Booker." One time, her introducer was heard to say "and here's the booker hooker herself…" For speaker and introducer, therein lies the trick of getting the title right, when it matters most.

Openings can be fraught with danger. Consider this experience of Toastmaster and professional speaker Michael J. Herman. On short notice, Herman was invited to fill in for an ailing speaker to address a professional society in San Diego on the subject of change. He thought the California Natural Society was hiring him. Michael prepared his presentation, drove down to San Diego, donned his best suit and, upon arrival at the presentation site, was met by his introducer and immediately ushered backstage. He was then introduced over the public address system.

Michael strode triumphantly onstage, shook the hand of his introducer, and then turned to the audience giving him a wonderful welcoming ovation. He immediately caught sight of a man in the front row, sans apparel. The man next to him was similarly disrobed. In fact the whole front row appeared to be naked. Michael thought he might be hallucinating. As he scanned the crowd he came to realize they were all nude! It turned out the group was the California Naturist Association, and they indeed were buck-naked.

Suddenly Michael felt overdressed. His first laugh of the day occurred when he asked if the audience would mind if he took off his coat. For years Michael had heard that a way to combat nervousness in public speaking situations involved imagining your audience had no clothes. For once, Michael tried imagining his audience had clothes. Michael confesses this was one time he was ambivalent about receiving a standing ovation.

Michael believes speakers should walk their talk. But this gig was different. Although his speech topic was "change," he himself was unwilling to change. In this case, he was happy to be overdressed.

Humor often derives from pronunciations, and mispronunciations. There was the speaker who was discussing the prevalence of stressed-out, type-A workers. She stated unequivocally that in Silicon Valley these workers were "You-Be-Qwee-shusss." Ubiquitous, or not, the laughter caused by her mispronunciation was ever-present in the meeting room.

Some of the funnier mispronunciations I've heard from the platform:

> LASH-a-Vicious (lascivious)
> Deeter-MINED (determined)
> Ana-THEEMA (anathema)
> Emer-EYE-tus (emeritus)

And my all-time favorite:

> Pair-ah-DIG-em! (for paradigm)

Toastmasters can take comfort in knowing that at every level of speaking, mispronunciations occur. While we want to say what we mean and mean what we say, it's nice to know our audiences appreciate the unintended humor when our minds say one thing, but our mouths say another.

So remember, perfect makes practice, I mean...well, you know what I mean, right?

A Funny Thing Happened On the Way to the Podium

Friends, Romans, Toastmasters, lend me your ears.
I bring you true tales from the stage of Shakespearean
proportions: drama, comedy, and mystery too.

In my seventeen years in Toastmasters I have seen some funny, funny things on the way to the podium. I bet you have too. Sometimes I laugh so hard it obscures valuable lessons found within the events. Consider some of the funnier scenes I've witnessed.

All Points Bulletin: Missing Target Speaker

There was once a Target, or Test Speaker, Steve, who left immediately after giving his speech instead of waiting to hear from the evaluation contestants. As contestants re-entered the room and began their evaluations, there was a telltale pause as they struggled, and failed, to find the target speaker in the audience. Finally, the last evaluator began with the customary "Thank you Madame Toastmaster, fellow Toastmasters, most welcome guests, and especially Steve...and promptly looked at me! Never mind that I wasn't the target speaker. The contestant needed someone to look at, and for the next three minutes he addressed me as if I were Steve. It worked with the judges; he won that night's contest.

Lesson learned: Sometimes continuity and the greater good is more important than drawing attention to a lapse, oversight or glitch.

Upstaged!

There was the time I was a guest speaker at another club and was scheduled to speak first. The second speaker, who planned to speak about dental hygiene, was sitting near the front. He was giving speech #9 wherein he would use props to make his point. While I was in the middle of my speech, I saw the other speaker fiddling with his props. Nonplussed, I continued. A few sentences later, one of his props, the electric toothbrush, sprung into action and started ambulating across the table, right in front of the lectern. In all my years of speaking I've been upstaged by coughers, sneezers, snoring, cell phones, pagers, fire alarms, crying babies, and even a minor earthquake tremor, but never an electric toothbrush.

Lesson learned: Some have a brush with death. I had a brush with distraction. As important as being unflappable, one must be unplaqueable.

Speaking Has Its Ups and Downs.

There was the time I attended my District's Leadership Breakfast at a local hotel that had a wooden stage built of risers. Our District Governor was doing a wonderful job of recognizing nominees for the President of the Term award. As was his style, he graciously invited each nominee to join him on the stage. Before we knew it, the stage was teaming with Toastmasters.

And then, just like that, whooosh! The entire stage collapsed. Luckily it was a two-foot drop and everyone on the stage remained standing. It was the funniest sequence of events: 20 people dropping straight down two feet and suddenly out of sight. Then 100 people in the audience rising up in unison to see what happened. Our focused District Governor, California Naturist Association in true Toastmaster fashion, never missed a beat. In fact, his humorous ad-libbing "set the stage" for the day's entertaining keynoter to follow.

Lesson learned: In life, it's less about what happens than how you handle it. A true leader is a situational leader. When no script exists, reflexes take over.

Smooth Sailing...NOT

Once every seven years, each District receives a visit from the International President. The president's visit to our District was my first opportunity to wear a tuxedo. In honor of the occasion, I actually bought a tux, special shirt, cummerbund and even shiny new tuxedo shoes. What a thrill it was to wear these items for the first time at our District's Spring Conference.

Midway through the evening's affair, my opportunity to speak arrived. I pushed back from my chair, rose, and regally ascended the stairs to the stage. This was the thrill of a lifetime; I was about to shake the hand of Toastmasters' International President. Then, very suddenly, as I was walking towards the VIP (visiting International President) to shake his outstretched hand, I slid into the splits. My brand new tuxedo shoes had bottoms so smooth I had lost traction. The entire head table gasped. Among 200 Toastmasters there was utter silence. The suspense was palpable. Would he arise? Could he aright himself? Alas I did, and the emcee said, "He slides...and is safe!"

> *Lesson learned: Sometimes one can be too smooth, or at least one's shoes can be too smooth! And many a mis-step can be adroitly corrected with a choice rejoinder.*

Coming Together

I'll never forget the time at our Regional Conference when an International Director was presenting an award to the conference chairwoman. The director gave the award recipient a hug...that didn't end. We knew there was mutual admiration, but the audience held its breath waiting for the two women to break their embrace. But they didn't. More accurately, they couldn't! The director's brooch had become hooked to the chairwoman's sweater. This gave new meaning to the phrase "I'm stuck on Toastmasters."

> *Lesson learned: Speakers should connect with their audiences, but not literally! We never know when we will be expected to maintain our poise and dignity. That night, both parties did, seemingly forever.*

Clues and Cues: Return to Sender

Then there was the time a past District winner of the International Speech Contest was asked to serve as a Target Speaker for an evaluation contest. To help the contestants, he deliberately committed numerous faux pas and intentional gaffes. His title was purposely off topic and his speech disorganized by design. His attire intentionally bore no relation to his theme. The evaluators would have a lot to work with. Instead, they complimented him on the very elements he had presented for their scrutiny. Imagine his surprise!

Lesson learned: Be authentic and let the chips fall where they may. Furthermore, it's easier to be good than to try to be bad.

Soon your District leaders will again be promoting upcoming contests and conferences. They will tell you about inspirational keynoters, wonderful educational sessions and other events being planned. What they can't tell you, what no one can tell you, are the unscripted, unexpected and unintended moments that offer both entertainment and wonderful learning opportunities. So keep your eyes and ears open, and soon you too will be telling audiences "A funny thing happened on the way to the podium!"

Toastmasters Do It...
Until They Hear Applause

What Laugh Lovers can teach us all about humor, comedy and punch lines

"Death is Easy...Comedy is Hard!"

Did you hear the one about the Speaker who tried to get the audience to laugh?

Let's face it, humor is hard! Toastmasters helps us overcome stage fright, speak to strangers and think on our feet. But seriously...being funny...on purpose?

We're adept at speaking to inform, persuading our audiences, and touching them with inspirational tales of love and loss. But how do we "break a leg" (a good thing in comedy parlance) by tickling our audience's funny bones? And why should we even try?

The truth is that speeches employing humor are better received. Audiences are more receptive when they've laughed. They relax, lower their defense mechanisms and become more open minded. Laughter causes them to connect more quickly with the speaker. But getting your audience to laugh...therein lies the challenge.

District 57 Toastmasters in Northern California formed a "comedy" club to help seasoned speakers become more proficient at the writing and delivering of humor. Meeting once a month in the San Francisco Bay Area, Laugh Lovers helps members learn about the art and science of humor. After all, we can all get an audience to laugh at us, but the key is understanding how to get them to laugh with us!

Laugh Lovers was inspired by the late John Cantu, a humorist and comedy coach who once managed the Holy City Zoo comedy club in San Francisco where comedians such as Robin Williams and Dana Carvey got their start. Back then, they too were learning to be funny. John relished the role of "humor helper" to comedians, fellow Toastmasters and members of the National Speakers Association worldwide. He believed we could all become funnier with practice plus an appreciation of the rules of comedy. Rules? Really! That's no joke.

Laugh Lovers carries on the tradition Cantu started in helping Toastmasters to be funnier. I recently interviewed Jeff Heidner, corporate humorist and former Laugh Lovers Toastmasters club president, about how Toastmasters can create and deliver funnier material. Below are Jeff's top ten tips for Toastmasters who want to be funnier.

1. **Be Yourself.** The world already has a Bill Cosby, Jay Leno and Ellen DeGeneres. It doesn't need another one. Yet there is room for your unique brand of humor. What's your brand? Finding it is your first assignment. Whenever you're conversing with people and you say something that makes them laugh, that's a clue! That's your unique brand of humor, the one you should use.

2. **Take Notes.** Whenever you say something that makes someone else laugh, write it down, literally. And don't forget to write down how you said it, and the context in which it was said. Otherwise, when you look back at your notes a

month later, you may find yourself wondering, "What was so funny about that?" Just the process of committing your amusing articulations to paper will go a long way towards helping you discover, develop and define your unique sense of humor.

3. **Pepper your speeches with humor.** Just as pepper spices up your favorite dish, you can (and should) use humor to season your speeches. Sprinkle humor into your next speech to grab the attention of your audience members. When used as an accent, humor adds just the right amount of flavor without overpowering everything else. Use humor to accent the important points in your speech, and your audience will remember the information long after the presentation.

4. **Special delivery recommended.** How you deliver your material is key. I've performed with many comedians who are talented writers yet they don't get laughs on stage. They get so frustrated when they see lesser comedy writers bringing the house down at will. Steps 5-7 offer delivery suggestions.

5. **Use your voice.** Toastmasters teaches us the importance of using vocal variety in our speeches. It's just as important, if not more so, when using humor. Change your inflection, use different characters and establish unique voices for each one. For added impact, go softer as well as louder when speaking. Doing so will help you create vivid images in the minds of your audience members and heighten the laughter you will garner.

6. **Timing is everything.** WARNING: Please pause prior to proceeding with the punch line. First of all, you need to

be sure your audience has digested the setup before your launch into the punch line. If they don't get the joke, you won't get the laughter. Secondly, by pausing for just a beat or two after your setup, you create that much more tension, and, consequently, you yield that much more laughter.

7. **Surprise.** Humor and tension go hand in hand. When you set up your audience for a moment of levity, you create tension. When you deliver the punch line—or the twist or surprise—you allow for that tension to be released. That release is manifested in the form of laughter.

8. **Stay clean.** No, I'm not talking about washing behind your ears. I'm talking about using humor that is appropriate for the audience you're addressing. Remember, humor is supposed to make people feel good—not embarrassed, insulted or offended. Stay away from comments that are sexist, racist, ageist, etc. Of course, if you want to make fun of yourself, go right ahead. Self-deprecating humor is a great way to put your audience at ease with you as a speaker so that they can get to know you as a person.

9. **Be Write-minded.** Write, rewrite and write some more! The more you think about your sense of humor, the more you take note of the funny things you say with your friends, the more you practice using your sense of humor in your speeches, the more comfortable you'll be with it. If your audience doesn't think your funny line is so funny, play with it, tweak it, rearrange it and try it again.

Have Fun. *That's a direct order! If you don't enjoy delivering it, then how can you expect an audience to laugh at it? Humor is contagious.*

Jeff, John and Craig agree on one more point:
Toastmasters, You Cantu Be Funny!

Craig and Jeff recommend:

1. Working Toastmasters' advanced speech manuals such as Humorously Speaking and The Entertaining Speaker will help you hone your humor skills.

2. Taking an Improv class. Like Table Topics, improvisational theatre will help you think and speak on your feet, appreciate audience dynamics, and overcome speaking fears through experimentation.

3. Use Table Topics as opportunities to create and relieve tension through humor, work on your timing and utilize the element of surprise for comedic effect.

4. Become a student of successful humorists, comedians and storytellers. Observe the histrionics of Bill Cosby, John Cleese and Carol Burnett. Study the timing of Cedric the Entertainer, Billy Crystal and Steve Martin. Analyze the mannerisms of stand up comedians such as Jay Leno and Whoopi Goldberg.

5. Admire the writing in television shows like M*A*S*H* and Seinfeld where many laughs are written into the dialogue.

6. Read and learn from a pair of our favorite free humor e-zines: John Kinde's Humor Power Tips (www.humorpower.com) and Karen Buxmon's Lytebytes (www.humorx.com).

7. Visit John Cantu's site, www.humormall.com, for a hefty helping of humor resources.

8. If you live in the Bay Area, and you're interested in attending a Laugh Lovers meeting, visit www.LaughLovers.us. If you're interested in creating a Laugh Lovers club for your District, then—you guessed it—e-mail Craig at Craig@LaughLovers.us.

Laugh Lovers Toastmasters club (596430-57) of Oakland CA was founded by DTMs and PDGs Craig Harrison and Cassandra Cockrill in honor of the late John Cantu, their dear friend. John was a Toastmaster and professional humor coach in and beyond the National Speakers Association. Visit www.HumorMall.com for more information on John Cantu.

Humor clubs abound. Craig recommends the following:

- ❖ When in Shanghai, PRC visit the Shanghai Humor Bilingual Toastmasters (998773-85)
- ❖ When in Brea (Orange County) California visit Humor Masters (1059533-Founders District)
- ❖ When in Waukesha, WI visit the Love of Laughter Toastmasters (1227778-35).

Jeff's Jocular Jargon for Toastmasters

By Jeff Heidner, CC

A BEAT – A unit of time that you measure by counting to yourself, to build suspense. Two beats equals the time it takes to say "One One Thousand, Two One Thousand."

CALLBACK – The art of reusing a word or phrase from a previous punch line to create new laughs in a different context.

COMEBACK – Material comedians write in advance to deal with hecklers just in case one appears and needs to be dealt with.

> "Thank you, but I prefer to work alone!"
> (May be followed by a *rim* shot: Ba Dum Tssshhh!)

HECKLER – An audience member, usually intoxicated, who interrupts a comedian's performance.

HOOK – If a comedian's act is so bad that it's hurting the show, a club owner may opt to "give him the hook" by yanking that comedian off of the stage prematurely as if using a giant hook.

PUNCH LINE – The phrase, line or word that releases the tension created in the set-up and garners laughter from the audience.

> Set-Up: "If I were two-faced…
> Punch Line: would I be wearing this one?"
> —*Abraham Lincoln*

The first phrase contains the *set-up* and the second phrase contains the *punch line*.

RIM SHOT – The proverbial drum/cymbal combination (ba-dum-bum-ting) that follows a painfully obvious or extremely corny joke or pun.

RULE OF THREE – Writing technique that creates a pattern with the first two items (set-up) and breaks that pattern with the third (punch line).

Example:

DIRECTIONS TO THE 2004 TOASTMASTERS INTERNATIONAL CONVENTION

1. Directions to Reno from West:
   Take Highway 80 East

2. Directions to Reno from East:
   Take Highway 80 West

3. Directions to Reno from Far East:
   Board a 747 bound for Las Vegas and then head north!

SAVER – A line used by a comedian to get a laugh after a previously delivered joke just bombed (usually self-deprecating).

SET-UP – The phrase or line that creates the anticipation and tension in an audience.

Corporate humorist Jeff Heidner was the 2004 president of Laugh Lovers (596430-57) of Oakland, CA. For more about Jeff visit www.havinghumorhelps.com.

How I Suffered From Foot-In-Mouth Disease

Sometimes I'm mellifluent, other times mistake-prone. Over the years, on my ascent from Competent Toastmaster to successful and respected motivational and humorous speaker, I've made my share of mistakes, malapropisms and misstatements.

Put another way, I am periodically afflicted with foot-in-mouth disease. But it's not for naught. There's much learning in one's foibles, as well as in others'. Laugh and learn from mistakes I've made as an emerging professional speaker.

Are You A Fluid Speaker?

When I first spoke at events and felt nervous beforehand, I would make sure to drink some cold water. At one particular event, my nerves threatened to overtake me altogether. I consumed glass after glass of cold water to quell my nervousness as I waited to be introduced. After five glasses of ice water, when I finally stood up to speak, I hardly recognized my own voice. It seems the cold water had constricted my vocal chords. *The lesson I learned that day: Make sure to drink warm or room temperature water or tea before speaking to loosen your vocal chords.*

As a new speaker, I often drank sodas before speaking on the theory that the sugar and caffeine rush would enhance my speaking. I learned the hard way that carbonated drinks seek a curtain call; they want to re-emerge from whence they came. On more than one occasion, a burp interrupted an important sentence uttered from the platform. I must say, amplified belches are the best argument against drinking carbonated beverages before speaking.

Another common mistake I made as an after-dinner speaker was eating a big meal before speaking. Convincing myself I needed all my energy for my big evening presentation, I gorged on a heavy meal of corned beef and cabbage, a baked potato with all the toppings, vegetables, a salad, rich chocolate cake and French bread. When I rose to speak, I did so haltingly. I felt sluggish and appeared bloated throughout the presentation. Clearly I had over-eaten. The truth is that adrenaline gives me the energy I had sought through carbonated tonics and meals. Overeating simply overtaxed my body at a time I needed to feel light and fluid. *Now, I will often arrange to eat my meal after I speak, when I am finally ready to dine in a leisurely and relaxed manner.*

You May Be On Without Being On Stage

As an emerging speaker, I partook of a Speakers Showcase at a trade show for meeting planners. The event showcases a number of speakers giving short presentations in rapid succession so the audience gets a glimpse of a series of speakers, subjects and styles. Backstage, speakers are constantly handing off microphones to the next speaker and mentally preparing for their moment in the spotlight.

Often there is a break between sets of speakers to give the meeting planners a chance to digest what they've seen, take a biological break, and otherwise stretch and relax. Through the luck of the draw, I was to be the first speaker after one such break. While the first five speakers gave their presentations, I waited nervously backstage to be fitted with a lavaliere microphone, which I had never used before. When the other speakers were done, I attached the microphone to my necktie, fed the cord inside my suit's jacket and clipped the cordless transmitter on my belt behind me. The sound tech flipped a switch and asked me to try it out: testing, testing, one-two-three. It worked. I was feeling pretty frisky!

He told me to return several minutes before the break ended and to enter from stage right upon being introduced. Suddenly I had ten minutes on my hand. How fortunate for me. I would go to the bathroom, and then find a quiet place to rehearse my opening one more time. I strode off to find a men's room. What luck to be able to relieve some of my nervousness. Then I entered the hallway, but there was nowhere to rehearse. Ah, I would duck outside to the sidewalk where I could speak loudly and not disturb anyone. As I rehearsed my opening, I made a few mistakes. Nervously, I chastised myself out loud. I repeated my opening until I finally nailed it. Praising myself with positive self-talk, I was ready to return to the auditorium.

As I returned, I learned that I really was one sought-after speaker. Why? My microphone transmitter had been on for the entire break. Everyone in the auditorium could hear me, but no one could find me to tell me to turn off the microphone. So much for my surprise opening! *Microphones often have an on-off or standby switch on them. Know your equipment and always make sure your microphone is in the off position before having backstage conversations and, especially, before going to the bathroom.*

When Confusion Reigns, It Pours

Memorizing has its place in speeches, to be sure. I have also found that over-memorization, and last minute cramming, can muddle a speaker's mind unnecessarily. I have spoken at District Conferences outside my own and accidentally referred by number to my District out of habit. Oops! It's an unintentional mistake that may be overlooked the first time. Just don't keep making that mistake, as I did.

Similarly, while in Canada I was speaking to a conference audience and relating a story of one of the attendees I had met the previous night. I was so focused on getting his name and its pronunciation correct that I mistakenly described him as being from Edmonton when, in fact, he was from Winnipeg. To this audience, my mistake turned out to be no little thing. Sometimes ignorance of local geography, customs or rivalries can have major consequences. *When speaking outside Toastmasters, know your localities, the organization you're speaking to, their product lines and who their chief competitor or rival is. You wouldn't praise Pepsi at a Coke Convention!*

Humor is Where *They* Find It

Sometimes in our quest to infuse humor in our material we forget that the best humor is what the audience finds funny. In many cases, it's not what we may have intended they laugh at. But let's not get in the way of our audiences having a good time.

For a customer service keynote to an audience of mortgage brokers, I extolled the virtues of professionals with a great "bedside manner," people who comfort customers, listen to them and, thus, uncover hidden needs. As an example, I contrasted two physicians I'd had. One came in, sat down, opened his laptop, started asking questions, and never even looked up to say hello or make any sort of contact. The other, my new physician, enters the examining room, smiles, greets me, and makes a modicum of small talk to relax us both. She uses questions to draw me out. I invited the audience to visualize our interaction with this sentence, "Can you see my doctor probing me?"

Well, before I could say another word, 170 mortgage brokers were laughing hysterically at the image of my physician literally probing me! I was speechless. My face turned red. I lost my train of thought. And they kept on laughing when they saw how flummoxed I was. But wait, we were bonding. This unexpected laugh was far more effective than some of my planned humor that morning. In fact, the rest of the speech went much better. *Let your audience decide what is funny. Sometimes it's the unexpected or unplanned situational humor that connects best. In a manner of speaking, run with it, not from it!*

The Fall and Rise of a Speaker

Sometimes there can be a language or cultural barrier between the speaker and an audience. I spoke once to a group of college students from Asia at a North American university campus. My topic was creativity and the spirit of invention. Most attendees that day weren't native English speakers. Since much of that presentation's humor was built around puns and word play, many of my jokes fell flat, my humor went unrecognized, and my confidence suffered. Then, while walking across stage in mid-sentence I tripped on the microphone cord and took a pratfall. The entire hall erupted in laughter. My stumble was hilarious to my audience. This was humor they recognized... slapstick. In my rush to resume my train of thought, I cut short their cathartic need to laugh. My mistake. After several more minutes of delivering dry material, I schemed to stage a second stumble, knowing that for this audience I could connect best through physical humor. *Be audience-centered! They determine what is funny. Tailor your humor to your audience and take your cues from them. Ultimately, humor is in the eye of the rejoicer.*

Band Aid to the Rescue

Toastmasters are called to speak in many capacities outside of the club. I have been pressed into service to make toasts at functions, to read proclamations at public events and also to serve as a Master of Ceremonies. It's a tribute to our skills and confidence level that others ask us to handle such important roles.

Several years ago I was invited to introduce a reggae band at a radio station fund-raiser. Since I was a fan of this band, this assignment was a particular treat. The previous band had vacated the stage, and my favorite band had set up and was ready to begin. All they needed was their formal introduction. The lights dimmed and the PA announcer introduced me, the chairman of the board for the radio station hosting the event. I came out onto a dark stage with the band members already at their instruments, poised to begin. A single spotlight shone on me. The smattering of applause was more to indicate the audience's excitement the show was continuing than any recognition of my importance.

I told the audience: "You are in for a big treat, this band is one of my favorites, they're local, they're talented and I want you to all put your hands together and give a big KKUP-FM radio station welcome to, the one, the only …"

And my mind went blank. I couldn't remember the band's name. At first the audience thought I was pausing for effect. I was frozen in the spotlight, unable to think and not knowing what to do. This band DID need an introduction. What was its name?

Suddenly, from behind me, I heard the drummer whisper in heavy Jamaican patois, "Raskidus, Mon!" As I privately thanked the Lord for this angelic drummer who saved the day, I blurted out "Raskidus Man" and ran from the stage. Raskidus was not amused. *In the heat of the moment you may have the potential to forget even the most basic information: who the audience is, the name of the event or the next presenter, etc. Make a note, carry a back-up crib sheet and avoid overtaxing your memory banks. Remember, an ounce of prevention is worth a pound of apologies.*

Don't Save the Best for Last

The best presentations seem to have powerful beginnings and endings and much in between to stimulate listeners. Especially for humorous speeches, it's important to have humor throughout.

I was hired to present a closing keynote at a software users conference held over a weekend in San Diego. My slot was Sunday morning, 10 a.m. until noon, following the president's remarks.

That morning the president spoke and then introduced me. I launched into my program. All went well for the first hour.

Then, in the middle of one of my stories, three people got up and quietly left. I pressed on. Ten minutes later an entire table of attendees got up and left. This was curious since their leaving seemed to bear no relationship to what I was saying.

Soon it was 11:45 am, time for my big close. The last fifteen minutes of my program had some of the best humor. Yet a mass exodus was occurring. Entire rows were vacating. There hadn't been an earthquake, a fire alarm or even a dirty diaper to induce such movement. Finally, as a few people near the front arose to leave I barked out, "Wait, you can't leave yet…you'll miss my big close." Sympathetically, a woman responded, "It's between missing your big close or my flight back to Minneapolis." Just then another man chimed in to remind everyone checkout time was noon. Suddenly, the entire room emptied. *You must be able to shorten your presentation on short notice. You may be competing against variables beyond our control: check out times, flight schedules, traffic and even alcohol. Insure your presentation contains value throughout, and have a back up plan in case your full time allotment to speak gets cut.*

Most days, I feel like a professional speaker, some days I feel like an emerging speaker or even like a submerging speaker. But each time out, I learn from the experience. May each of you avoid foot-in-mouth disease as you develop as speakers.

Toastmasters Haikus

Just as Toastmasters speak within time limits, we can learn to write within word limits too. Haikus are a popular form of Japanese poetry known for their brevity. Haikus are non-rhyming poems of just three lines, with the first and third lines consisting of five syllables each, and the middle line containing seven syllables. The following Haikus were inspired by my seventeen years with Toastmasters.

A case of bad nerves
The beginning speaker's fate.
Time to sip sake.

                        I love Toastmasters!
                Members who care, programs too
                           Give me Confidence

I entered with fear,
Then Toastmasters worked with me…
Listen now: they clap!

                          Communication
                Is why I joined Toastmasters…
                        Now I'm a Leader.

Joined to help myself—
In clubs I help many more
To speak and lead well.

                        Learning CAN be Fun.
                Dr. Smedley knew the way.
                    Ergo Toastmasters.

Each speech that I give
Counts as a manual speech.
My EVP smiles.

A World that speaks well.
What a great vision to have.
Toastmasters does it!

> In contests we find
> Speeches can't go forever.
> Limits can be good.

Gavel bangs each week.
Another meeting begins
And will end on time.

> WHQ[1]
> The people we never see
> Phyllis? Voice I love.

What is a PerCap?
I can be one, two or three
My District keeps track.

> Conventions are great
> Yearly extravaganzas
> Next year: Palm Desert!

Everybody wins
Through the Toastmasters programs—
Group recognition!

> Service Leadership
> The backbone of Toastmasters…
> Please accept when asked.

Join a club and get
Raises, promotions and more;
How can you resist?

> Joined to speak better
> Now I teach others the same
> Mom, look at me now!

---

1. WHQ stands for World Headquarters in Rancho Santa Margarita, California, USA.

Good, Better...BEST!

Ums and Ahs I had
Now without them I have found
More time for real words.

                    Speak with Confidence.
                    It's easy when your guide is
                    Toastmasters each week.

Me? Shy and reserved.
Now, called to speak in public.
Praise to Toastmasters!

                    The Word-of-the-day?
                    You say: Transformational
                    I'll Show What You Mean.

Clubs around the World
Toastmasters—it is like the
United Nations!

                    Many men, women
                    Join together every week
                    To make their voice strong!

Dues are due again.
Just twice a year do we pay
For year-long learning.

                    My mailman arrives.
                    With The Toastmaster in tow.
                    Now he may join too!

With Pins and Ribbons
I dress for the success of
Our Spring Conference!

                    Build a club they say.
                    Help other folks speak better
                    Via Toastmasters!

Timer she shows Green
More to say, seeing Yellow
Done in Time...No Red!

We do more than talk
We listen and lead as well
What a great program.

I aspire to
Be the World Champion
Just six wins to go!

Shake my hand and sit
But don't go too far away...
(First Table Topic)

Evaluate me
To motivate me and more
So we can all learn.

Youth Leadership is
My most favorite program.
Young people learn fast!

Contagious clapping
A hallmark of our meetings
Makes us all feel great!

Mentoring others
It's a great feeling to share
And help others grow!

To have speaking skills
Gives us all special powers
Now, make a difference!

"Mr. Toastmaster
Fellow Toastmasters and Guests"
Say I to begin...

"Shake my hand" she says
But it's already shaking!
—It's my Ice Breaker.

A master of toasts
And a teller of tales
We wear many hats.

> I just cannot lie—
> Life was one moment of truth
> Until joining up.

Me: From fear to fun;
You: Can aspire and achieve;
We can both succeed.

> Santa Ana winds
> Blow words around the world
> Dr. Smedley smiles.

Postscript: Try your hand at a Haiku. Each has three lines. The first and third lines should contain five syllables. The middle line should contain seven. Challenge yourself to include some aspect of the environment in yours!

_____ _____ _____ _____ _____

_____ _____ _____ _____ _____ _____ _____

_____ _____ _____ _____ _____

E-mail your HAIKU for a special reward:

Craig@ExpressionsOfExcellence.com

The Communication Conundrum

You just don't understand!
I thought you meant the opposite.
What are you saying?

Sound familiar? Mercury doesn't have to be in retrograde for miscommunications to ensue. At times it's as common as conversation itself to have disagreement and misunderstandings.

Reading haikus can be comforting. Writing them can be therapeutic. Research haikus for yourself and appreciate this Japanese art form. Try your own hand at a haiku, a three-line poem whose first and third lines each have five syllables and whose second line has seven. Traditionally, haikus have a connection to their environment as well. Yours can, too.

The topic for these haikus: communication!

Like ships in the night
Our past communications…
We spoke Pier-to-Pier

> He says and she says
> Shared thoughts, different styles
> Each has its value

Cell phones in public
Why must you yell to be heard?
Whisper or I'll scream!

Good, Better...BEST!

I asked for the bill.
Your hat hit me in the face.
Send the manager.

                        Yes, yes you nodded.
                     I thought you agreed with me.
                          You simply heard me.

A motion was made.
When you then seconded it
'Twas for its defeat!

                               Erratic driver,
                  Not drunk, just preoccupied.
                         Just hang up and drive!

Passionate speaker
Says she yells because she cares,
I like the 'soft' sell.

                          Both your lips quiver.
               It seems I have struck a nerve.
                   Sometimes spit happens.

My boss says he cares.
Another birthday ignored.
Does he know I'm here?

                             Another meeting:
                So much pain, so little gain
                 Too much "meet" is bad!

"We must talk" you shout!
I feel I'm being attacked
Speak with me instead.

                      Rudeness is your way
          Not the best for building teams.
                    Go work for yourself!

Generous with blame
Your focus is on others.
Look in the mirror.

Credibility:
For those who can walk their talk.
Learn it and earn it.

                    Learning to say No.
                    My self-respect is rising.
                    Now I'm in the know.

Communication
It's fraught with much potential
For better or worse.

                    Customer's happy!
                    I advocated for him.
                    Loyalty was won.

Synchronicity
Two people with the same thoughts
Did she read my mind?

                    A first-time caller...
                    Talk radio at its best.
                    First please turn yours down!

It's unethical!
He took credit for my work.
My Boss—not for long.

                    Gentle and friendly
                    She listened with care, concern.
                    The language of love.

Now for fun, collaborate with a colleague or co-worker to write haikus about your success, pet peeve or recent experience. Managers, sponsor a haiku contest to express departmental themes.

I AM AFRAID TO SPEAK!

Homage to Toastmasters…and Dr. Seuss

I am afraid to speak
I am I am
But do I get help?
Noooooo, I sit home on my can

>It's true, it's true
>I am afraid to SPEAK
>I'm Mr. Whisper and most call me Meek

I Mumbled, I Bumbled, I Stumbled I did
in an Adult World I appeared like a Kid

>Yes, I had a fear
>Or should I say it had me
>And worst than that
>It was one all could see

Of strangers I was afraid
New friendships: never made
Fun outings…I did shun
Social settings made me run.

>Fear made me small
>Fear made me weak
>Yet God gave me voice
>With intent I would speak

I could sing in the shower
of that I was able
But in groups I did cower.
I'd hide under the table.

> I needed help
> Woe was me
> Yet the answer was here
> and it fit me like a "T"

My fear was my downfall
it was potentially deadly
but my struggle wasn't unique
Heck, it started before Smedley.

> I was at a crossroads
> Which way would I turn
> To be a confident speaker
> There was much to learn

So I became a Toastmaster
now I'm the Cat with the plan
I'm working my manuals
I am winning new fans

> I replaced Fear with Fun
> When I joined my first club
> I made new friends…
> the Club became my Hub

I gave a speech a month
I did, I did!
And at work I did speak
where before I had hid

> I entered a contest
> I won! I won!
> I went to my first District Conference
> and my was it FUN!

At TLI I learned to be
a better speaker & leader
As the Very Reverend Verbal T. Toastmaster,
I became a Preacher

      I became a District Leader,
    and spread the Gospel of Toastmasters
       I saw potential in others
     and became an astute forecaster

Green Eggs and Ham may be for Seuss
But for me, Green lights and certificates
are of much more use

      Now I don't like to brag
      And I don't like to boast
     But of all the folks I've met
    I like Toastmasters the most!

Because Toastmasters are really cool cats
Toastmasters wear many hats

    WordMaster, JokeMaster, TopicMaster Too,
   Something for Me and Something for You!

Toastmasters are really cool cats
Some Toastmasters wear other hats

     At Conferences and Conventions
      they campaign and vote
   As Sponsors & Mentors they coach & dote

So join a club, give manual speeches
and head Straight for Success
You're destined for greatness
Accept nothing less

Through Speech we can Touch,
We can Teach. We can Reach.
We can Praise and be Praised
I like to do each!

NOW IT'S YOUR TURN:
WON'T YOU DO YOUR PART?

YES, Help others in need
Turn Their Fear into Fun
Start new clubs so even more
'fraidy cats can come

AND REMEMBER…
If I can do it ,
you can too!
Together we triumph.
Until then, Adieu!

Good, Better...BEST!

IV. STORYTELLING

Storytelling predates writing. Indeed, the oral tradition is one of our oldest traditions. And it's still one of the best ways to teach, transmit, educate, entertain, inspire and motivate others. That's why storytelling and Toastmasters go hand in hand.

Master storytelling and you will be more effective at work, at home, in relationships and wherever you communicate. As you will read in this section, you can tell tales in and out of school, at work and even in other countries. You can participate in the worldwide tradition of storytelling. Best yet, you will live happily ever after!

Good, Better...BEST!

Become a Storyteller...
Two Minutes at a Time!

Don't look now, but you're surrounded...by stories. Everywhere you look and listen, stories are being told, retold and even created.

Our Storied Past

Growing up, we were told stories by our parents, grandparents, favorite uncles or aunts. That's how we learned about our rich family history and ethnic heritage, whether around the dinner table or the kitchen table, the fireplace, front stoop or back porch.

Our parents and babysitters used stories to put us to sleep at night. Whether they read tales from books, told family stories passed down through generations, or made up stories to suit our fancy, stories instilled values, pride and an understanding of how the world worked. Stories helped us envision what was possible, and cautionary tales told us what not to do!

In school, we studied stories, whether about the building of our nation, Greek mythology or Shakespeare's classics. After school and on weekends, we learned stories of our religious heritage. Summer camps were full of stories. As were fishing and camping trips. And of course, we as kids told tales out of school! We were natural storytellers.

Novels, radio programs, TV shows, movies and newspapers are also full of stories, each with exotic settings, fascinating characters, incredible journeys, seemingly unconquerable obstacles and fantastic triumphs of epic proportions. Even opera, rap and commercials are further examples of stories, expertly told, that connect with others.

Relocating the Storyteller in You

As we get older, we learn new ways of imparting information: the essay, the résumé, the elevator speech, job interview, the meeting report. Meanwhile, our storytelling skills atrophy. The good news: relief is just a Toastmasters meeting away. I recommend you start by telling two-minute stories in the form of responses to weekly Table Topics.

Two-Minute Tales

What are the elements of a story: setting, characters, action, and reaction all leading to a resolution. You can cover all of that, in style, in two minutes, and even receive applause for your effort. And don't underestimate the power of an archetypal story—a story whose theme, structure or feel we seem to know instinctively. Those tales connect the best!

And the Topic is...

Here are some examples of topics you might receive and how your response can take the form of a story:

Why is Bike Safety Important?

Answer this topic with a story of you as a biker (or driver). Cycle through the scenario, action and outcome. Color the topic with descriptive language. The whoosh of the car, jarring of the pothole, the smell of car exhaust in the bike lane, etc.

The Vacation from Hell…

Take us with you as you revisit the vacation from hell. The misery, monotony or malady that overwhelmed your best-laid plans. Give us a travelogue with sounds, smells, moods and local color.

The First Kiss

We want to hear the love story that blossomed…in school, after school or at summer camp. The tension, anticipation and ecstasy involved with the buss. Let us hear your heart beating, smell the sweat and hear the music as you kiss for the first time.

The Ghost Story

Weave a yarn about a haunted house or other location where spirits dwell. Give us suspense, fear and trepidation. Let us hear the voices, see the apparitions and suspend reality as you conjure up scary monsters.

Your Favorite Pet

A love story if ever there was one. Anthropomorphize. Tell us the most human elements of your relationship with Fifi, Fido or Fredo.

Your Favorite Meal or Food

Take us dining with you. Relive the meal or special occasion. Help us breathe in the savory smells, taste the succulent dishes and sate all our senses with your story. Give us the anticipation beforehand and the satisfaction that follows. We'll digest it all as you tell it.

Stories Speak

According to storyteller Jean Ellison, co-director of the Bay Area Storytelling Festival: "Stories speak! Among the benefits of story and storytelling: to remind us how to listen. If we could just be better listeners, we'd reduce our workplace quarrels, interpersonal strife, and globally the world would be a more peaceful place." We, as Toastmasters can do our part, two minutes at a time.

Two-Minute Warning!

Scour your kitchen for an egg timer and use it to practice your two-minute stories. (Remember, in Table Topics you have up to 2 ½ minutes! Leave a little sand in the glass.)

When you're next called for Table Topics, think "story" instead of speech or stream of consciousness. Whatever the topic, you can likely tell a two-minute story, replete with a locale, characters, a challenge and a triumph. As 85-year old Toastmaster and storyteller Orunamamu often tells her Lakeview Toastmasters (2767-57) in Oakland, CA:

> "I stepped on a pin, the pin bent,
> "And that's the way the story went."

Well, what are you waiting for? It's story time!

Storytellers and Toastmasters: *Learning from Each Other*

Storytellers and Toastmasters. Similarities abound. Each communicates with audiences, entertains, informs and inspires their listeners, and receives applause in return. Storytelling is arguably the oldest profession, and its traditions carry on around the world.

For their part, Toastmasters have been meeting since 1924 when founder Ralph C. Smedley launched the educational non-profit now with over 10,000 clubs in over 90 countries. There are already Toastmasters clubs dedicated to storytelling in Districts around the world, and Toastmasters conferences and conventions with sessions on this art form. *Toastmasters* magazine features articles about storytelling. There are even storytellers who are active Toastmasters using club meetings to polish their craft and develop new material.

As one who is active in both communities, I've come to believe each group has valuable lessons to teach the other.

Five things Toastmasters can learn from Storytellers:

1. Vocal Variety

Stories feature characters, each with their own voices. Tellers develop the ability to distinguish different characters for their audiences through their vocal inflections, variety, pitch, volume, accent and nuances.

For your next speech, instead of describing dialogue, deliver it using different voices for each participant.

2. Stage Presence

Many Toastmasters find themselves tethered to a lectern, planted in front of a microphone or behind a table. They rarely make full use of the stage or podium. Storytellers will often use the entire stage—coming upstage, downstage, to the left or right, to say nothing of kneeling, teetering and more.

Expand your speaking platform. Own the stage area and use it to further your presentation. Inhabit your environment.

3. The Power of the Pause

Storytellers understand the pause as a valuable mechanism for building drama, adding suspense, and imbuing key words and sentences with added meaning. Pauses signify to audiences that something profound, important or special has been—or is about to be—said.

Review your speech's script or outline and look for key spots to introduce pauses for heightened effect!

4. Imagery

Storytellers excel at details that add to the power of a piece. Storytellers paint marvelous verbal images of scenes and settings: the sights, smells and sounds, the nuances and subtleties of situations and all the specifics. They use adjectives to convey color and detail in their stories. Often Toastmasters give us just the facts, and little else.

Use imagery evocatively to enrich your speech, table topic or opening/closing thought.

5. Setting the Stage

Every story is different. Thus, each time a storyteller takes the stage or begins a story, he or she has a blank canvas on which to paint. Like Toastmasters, they "paint" through body language, gestures, facial expressions and vocal variety. They don't rely on the clichéd "Mr./Madame Toastmasters, fellow Toastmasters and most welcome guests…" opening line. Toastmasters who rely on this rote opening are relying on a crutch that doesn't work beyond Toastmasters meetings. Worse yet, it undercuts any impact a powerful opening line or paragraph possesses.

Toastmasters can begin each presentation by setting the stage appropriately—though posture, voice, gestures, and employing other elements like surprise, shock, mystery or suspense.

Five things Storytellers can learn from Toastmasters

1. Speaking "In the Moment"

Toastmasters regularly participate in Table Topics, where they're asked to speak "off the cuff" for 1-2 minutes on a random topic without any preparation time. As a result, they become adept at thinking, listening and speaking on their feet and reacting to whatever comes their way.

This skill can help storytellers with their pre-, post- and between-story interactions with audiences, as well as when the unexpected occurs: a cell phone rings or the Norfolk Southern Railway train passes nearby and toots its horn.

2. The Value of the Introduction

Toastmasters pride themselves on mastering the art of the introduction. They delight in introducing each other in ways that draw in audiences, predispose them to listen, build credibility in the presenter and foreshadow the presentation to come.

Audiences are naturally curious about tellers too. Your introduction can help audiences get to know, appreciate and admire you and deepen their connection to you and your stories.

3. Developing One's Internal Time Clock

Toastmasters time all aspects of their meetings, with special attention to speeches. Their contests are won (or lost) in part through adherence to prescribed time limits. Whether they are giving a 5-7 minute speech, a 2-3 minute evaluation or speaking "off the cuff" for 1-2 minutes, the net result is that they, over time, develop an excellent ability to measure presentation time. Thus they become more adept at the ability to perform for a finite amount of time, no more and no less.

Each week Toastmasters practice speaking within time limits. Storytellers too can develop a feel for how to tell a two-minute tale, a seven-minute story or something in between.

4. Live Audiences

Toastmasters provide their members with a ready-made audience. Tellers can benefit from an audience of poised listeners who laugh, sigh and cry in response to what they hear. How wonderful for tellers! Oh, did I mention Toastmasters' proclivity for clapping? Tellers can practice in isolation only so much.

As Tellers, we can use audiences to refine our material, fine-tune our timing and gauge audience comprehension, appreciation and reaction.

5. Immediate Feedback

Toastmasters evaluate all presentations. They are skilled at acknowledging strengths and recommending areas for improvement. Their blend of motivation and specific recommendations provide tellers with immediate feedback on what was effective and where improvement can occur.

Tellers can gather many data points about their stories through the written and verbal evaluations Toastmasters provide each meeting.

Untold Stories – Misnomers on Both Sides

Just as many presume storytelling is just for kids, so too do many people regard Toastmasters as simply those that are afraid to speak. In point of fact, storytelling is for everyone, and Toastmasters holds value for beginners and advanced orators alike.

This Story Is To Be Continued…

What are you waiting for? This story doesn't end here. You're the central character in this story. It's your move. Find a specialty club in your District that emphasizes storytelling. If there isn't one, e-mail; I'll help you build one! There is an existing storytelling community just waiting to connect with you.

Once Upon a Job...

"Success" Stories Help Job Seekers Sell Their Skills!

Nothing succeeds like success, according to the old French proverb. And for job seekers, nothing succeeds quite like *success stories*. Are you sharing yours? If not, why not?

As a Toastmaster, you're already skilled at telling short stories. You do it every week during Table Topics. *Success stories* are thirty- and sixty-second stories that can be shared in job interviews, at networking events or even socially in casual conversation.

While your résumés' bullets and dashes accurately tell a reader what you've done, *success stories* tell a listener so much more. Did you know you had a storied past?

During interviews, a quick-hitting story can make or reinforce a point in memorable fashion. *Success stories* may be told in response to a question, to punctuate a credit on a résumé, or even as an aside. They can showcase your acumen, demonstrate your facility with others or profile your leadership qualities.

Each story shows you succeeding in a work context, which is the purpose of your interview. Remember, the person interviewing you is trying to envision how you'll do in their work environment. Past performance is often the best predictor of future success, so it behooves you to share your successes. Stating just dry facts or statistics leaves interviewers cold. Telling your story adds the color, context and realism to help your interviewer appreciate your skills and experience and how you applied them. Success stories showcase your values, qualities and thought processes while telling listeners how you achieved these accomplishments.

Stories work for several reasons. For starters they're more memorable than numbers, names and dates. Stories also work well because we enjoy the drama: a problem followed by a solution, a mystery solved with a twist, or a creative workaround to a seemingly insurmountable obstacle. Also, the listener can find him or herself in the story as well. A good story will resonate with listeners.

According to Gay Ducey, a past president of the National Storytelling Network, "We're wired for stories, individually and collectively. Since the time of Odysseus we've been told stories. Since we were little kids we've been read and told stories. This is how we've been conditioned to learn; our morals and our values are taught through stories." So our connection with listeners is an emotional one as well.

Look at your résumé and pick out an accomplishment. Now tell your interviewer the story behind the accomplishment. If your résumé states that you increased sales 60%, tell how you did it; Give us a "before vs. after" description. What was the secret? Stories that reveal secrets captivate their listeners.

Your curriculum vitae indicates you streamlined production time 40% in your last job. What was the key to this success? Why hadn't others done this already? What personal quality helped you succeed at this task where others before you hadn't?

The Three S's of Success Stories

Success stories offer a setting, a situation and a solution. Remember, you're the hero of your stories. Your decisions, actions and insights made a difference, and it's OK to say so. You don't have to be boastful, but make the late sportscaster Howard Cosell proud: "Tell it like it is!"

Here is an example of how one candidate used storytelling to summarize his most recent employment for a competitor:

> "In my last job, I was hired to manage a production department at war with the editorial department. I walked into an environment full of distrust and resentment built up over years of animosities and recriminations. Through my implementation of cross training between departments, initiation of mutual social outings such as picnics and scheduling of project post-mortems we were able, after 6 months, to convert resentment into understanding and competition into cooperation. As each department began to understand how the other one worked, we were jointly able to improve the workflow and consequently shorten time to market with publications. Even quality improved as we better understood how best to work together. That showed me the importance of internal company communication and how hard it can be, though not impossible, to change an existing culture.

Not only does this success story demonstrate the candidate's ability to solve problems, it also shows interviewers the candidate's understanding of inter-office politics and the human side of operations. This candidate took initiative, was a change agent and didn't shy away from a challenge. Notice how the same story can convey multiple qualities.

Stories can demonstrate your detail orientation, dedication, leadership, independence, researching ability, creativity or problem solving skills. Remember that employers want well-rounded hires, so make sure they see evidence of your varied skill set. Here are a few examples:

- ❖ Your conversion of old equipment into new uses shows you can think outside the box and are resourceful.

- ❖ Coming up with non-monetary ways to recognize your staff shows your creativity and leadership by demonstrating that you understand how to motivate others.

- ❖ The weekly internal E-letter you created for employees not only boosted morale, it offers proof of your strong communication skills.

- ❖ The canned food drive you initiated at your last job not only showed your commitment to your community, it also raised visibility for the company and improved their public relations.

- ❖ By forming a lunchtime jogging club, you helped bring employees from different departments together while improving the physical and mental health of employees who participated. Your leadership and team building skills were further evidenced when your runners club formed a Centipede in the recent Bay to Breakers race.

- ❖ Your multilingual skills helped aright a project suffering from miscommunication between subsidiaries from overseas. Not only could you translate phrases and idioms of speech, your insight into cultural differences bridged a gap and corrected a wayward project. More than showcasing your knowledge of languages, you demonstrated the ability to liaison between different groups, negotiate and turn an important project around.

Review your past work history and identify the stories within each accomplishment. Now tell it to others. Make sure you include the moral to your story. What is the ultimate point that the story makes about you, your skills and credits?

When employers hire candidates with such skills and experience, new success stories will emerge. Your continued employment makes yours a never-ending story. And remember, it's never too soon to tell your story. It always begins with "Once upon a job…"

Toastmaster Success Stories Reap Recruiting Rewards

There was a setting you found yourself in, a situation you experienced and success was the final result. Voila! You have a success story! Many Toastmasters share their membership success stories, and, in the process, enroll others in their clubs. After all, success is contagious!

Why did you join Toastmasters? What was your aim? To learn to speak in public? Sharpen your leadership skills? Speak confidently off-the-cuff? Improve your vocabulary?

When you share your Toastmasters success story with others, they naturally see what Toastmasters could do for them, too. Your personal testimonial becomes more powerful than any brochure or website in showing guests what awaits them when they join Toastmasters.

My story? Toastmasters transformed me from a mumbling, fumbling, stumbling whisperer into a confident communicator—so much so that I am now a professional speaker. Toastmasters has turned my fear into fun, and I've seen it change others' lives too. If it can help me, it can help you!

Think about your story. Other people you know may already be telling it! They have seen the "before and after" difference since you joined Toastmasters. Paint the picture! What has opened up for you as a result of your Toastmasters membership? A new career? A promotion? The confidence to form or join a social group? Did you run for office? Did you meet your spouse through Toastmasters? Tell others your special story, and they'll begin to understand what is available to them through our marvelous organization.

Stories abound. Once you've fashioned yours, think about others who've joined your club since you have. What does their success story sound like? I've seen shy and timid newcomers later become top officers, contest winners and master recruiters. I recount their stories to others as well. It's amazing what confidence and a taste of success can do.

Become a teller of Toastmaster tales. Tell the world of your success, and soon they'll be knocking at your club's door for a taste of their own success. And we'll all live happily after!

Tips for Telling

1. Use vocal variety, gestures and body language to reinforce your story's words

2. Tell your story in a conversational tone

3. Use pauses for effect

4. Give eye contact to convey your sincerity

5. Paint vivid pictures and add color with adjectives

6. Tap universal themes: overcoming obstacles, the hero's journey, a search for solutions, etc.

7. Use confidence derived from Toastmasters to showcase your strong communication skills.

From Silk to Story:
Tellers and Toastmasters Trade Threads of Traditions Through Visit to China

The Peoples' Republic of China remains a country steeped in tradition, yet clearly in transition. On a 2007 trip with forty other professional storytellers from across the U.S., this Toastmaster experienced the old and the new during three weeks in China.

Storytelling – Bridging the Continental Divide

We visited Gengcun, an impoverished rural village dating back to the time of the old Silk Road. Gengcun boasts a 600-year tradition of storytelling. Among its 1,200 residents are more certified storytellers than any other location in China. Some are master tellers who know over 100 stories!

With the help of two levels of interpreters, our English stories were translated, first into Mandarin, then into the local dialect. For almost a week, the other visitors and I told and heard stories among 3rd and 4th grade students in their school, in the homes of village tellers, and in their Hall of Stories.

When not telling stories in and out of school, we engaged in art and music projects, dancing and joining in celebrations at their local shrines.

Story Threads

From local tellers, we heard stories about dragons, turtles, monkeys and elephants, about evil step-mothers and precocious children, mischievous dogs, emperors and dowagers, love unrequited and love reciprocated. Many of their stories echoed stories we'd heard of Persian, Native American, African, European and Russian origin.

Many of our stories had Chinese variations as well. Despite differences in language, it was fascinating to hear the story of the three little pigs in Chinese, to simultaneously enjoy the immediacy of a mime's routine, and to use facial and body gestures and smiles honed in Toastmasters meetings to connect with foreigners on their own soil.

Watch Your Tone!

In the Chinese language intonation is everything. We learned that the sound "ma," depending on its tone, could have five different meanings, from mother to hemp to horse and beyond!

Inflection informs meaning. Many of the stories hinged on subtleties of language—puns and dual meanings of words based on tone. Humor came in waves as these subtleties were revealed through translations. Other differences abounded. We learned about Chinese lucky numbers (eights are very popular), Feng Shui and the significance of certain colors.

Tellers and Toastmasters Unite

Another highlight of our trip was a visit with eight other storytellers to Beijing #1 Toastmasters (#6126-U) on September 11. There, our tellers told 90-second stories and engaged as a panel in a question and answer session with members who spoke English as a second or third language. One teller, 14 year-old Chloe Clunis, dazzled Toastmasters with her prowess for her age; Colorado teller Anita Strickbine spoke poignantly about how her father's life and hers were both changed through Toastmasters when he joined a club in Germany almost 50 years earlier while serving in the U.S. Army. Yours truly shared experiences of departing the People's Republic of Berkeley as an expert in communications only to be humbled by a lack of comprehension on arrival in the P.R.C.

The Laugh Heard Halfway Around the World

Most exciting for this Toastmaster was the realization that a specialty club I chartered in the San Francisco Bay Area to focus on humor, Laugh Lovers (596430-57), has inspired similar clubs in Beijing and Shanghai! Humor really is a universal language.

Toastmasters Paving the Way

Nowhere is Toastmasters growing as rapidly as in China. Through promotion of communication and leadership skills, it is leading its own cultural evolution that contributes to China's key role in our current world.

You probably saw and heard a lot about China during its date with destiny as host of the 2008 Summer Olympics. I encourage you to prepare to experience for yourself all that is China in the twenty-first century.

To read more stories about this storytelling exchange between storytellers in the US and the PRC, visit these online articles of Craig's:

www.ExpressionsOfExcellence.com/ARTICLES/ NSN Jan-Feb NuWa_article.pdf

www.ExpressionsOfExcellence.com/ARTICLES/Storytellers_in_China.pdf

www.ExpressionsOfExcellence.com/ARTICLES/Silk_to_Story.pdf

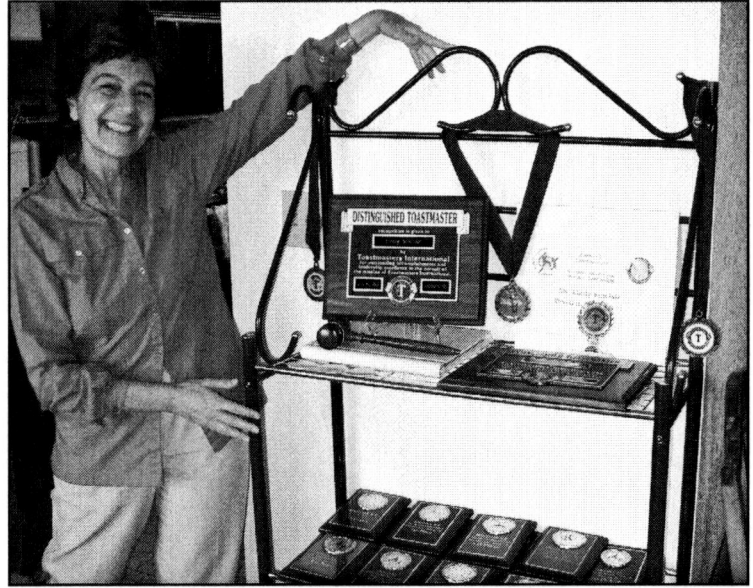

Lindy Sinclair DTM of D-57 shares a few of her emblems of excellence.

V. EXCELLENCE

Consummate Toastmasters are on a never-ending journey of self-improvement. Each meeting, each speech and indeed in each leadership or meeting role, Toastmasters strive to be better than the last time. They look for opportunities to shine. They continuously express excellence.

Applying the Japanese concept of *Kaizen*, Toastmasters look to improve in large and small ways. Remember, little things make the difference, although the difference is no little thing. Toastmasters who apply the following tips and suggestions for self-improvement will ultimately develop mastery as communicators and leaders.

Good, Better...BEST!

Expressions of Excellence!

Ample Ways of Exuding Excellence Through the Toastmasters Experience

Do you express your excellence each time you participate in a Toastmasters event? Here's why you can, and should, express your excellence, regardless of your role, at every meeting, contest, conference and training. Our inspiration for excellence: the late Joe DiMaggio.

"Joltin" Joe DiMaggio was as fine a baseball player as ever was. A Hall of Famer and two-time batting champ, the Yankee Clipper, as he was known, set the record for the longest hitting streak in major league history—56 games! His mark may never be broken. Joe DiMaggio exemplified excellence.

Late one summer, when the Yankees were already a cinch for the World Series, Joe was banged up. He had bumps and bruises from a season of running, sliding, diving for balls and being hit by pitches. There was no need for him to even be in the lineup, let alone play 100% all-out in this particular game. And yet, there he was, taking the extra base on a base hit, running full speed, sliding into the bag in a cloud of dust.

After the game, a sportswriter asked him why he was playing so hard in such a meaningless game. Joe looked at him and answered in all earnestness: "Because someone might be seeing me play for the very first time!"

That's an expression of excellence!

Joe DiMaggio's pride in his appearance and in his reputation was so important that for Joe it meant never taking a day off. It meant always giving his best performance.

Do you strive to make every speech your best yet? If not, why not? As a speaker, do you treat all your audiences to your best? Or do you calibrate your performance to the number of people in the room?

Don't ration your excellence. If you stand for excellence, then don't apportion it out in relation to who you believe is in the audience or whether your audience is big or small. Whether there are two, twenty or two hundred in your audience, they deserve the best you can offer. As a seventeen-year Toastmaster and current professional speaker, each time out I strive to express my excellence. I treat every presentation as if I were competing in the World Championship of Public Speaking!

Here's Looking For You!

I spoke at a meeting that, as a result of an unexpected location change, had just one other person in attendance. It would have been easy to feel sorry for myself and cancel the speech or suddenly not care and give a sub-par performance. I'll admit I felt funny saying "Mr. Toastmaster, Fellow Toastmaster, and missing members..." yet I saw this as a challenge in and of itself. True, I had some fun with this situation, asking the other attendee (who was concurrently the Toastmaster, my entire audience and speech evaluator), "Can you hear me in the back?" But P.T. Barnum was right: the show must go on!

To Be Continued...

Modeling excellence should be a full-time endeavor. If you embrace the Japanese concept of kaizen—continuous improvement—then you understand that each time you speak off the cuff, give a prepared speech or introduce or evaluate another speaker, you have the opportunity to model excellence. Each utterance can be an expression of excellence. And when you express your excellence, it not only advances you, it inspires others, too.

CCs: Competence to Mastery

As a Distinguished Toastmaster and Advanced Leader, it would be easy for me to believe I've topped out. Yet, each year I complete another CC for Districts 4 and 57, where my home clubs are located, because I believe I can express my excellence through completing the basic manual whether for the first or ninth time. And each year I learn more as I repeat this seminal manual. It's one of my expressions of excellence.

Multiple Expressions

Interestingly, you can express excellence without uttering a word. A Sergeant-at-Arms whose meeting room is well set up, the Toastmaster of the day's well designed meeting agenda, the tastefully dressed and groomed attendee who makes a positive impression on a guest—each is an expression of excellence demonstrating good taste, good planning and good manners. When you strive for excellence, you find ample opportunities to express it. So, whether your name is Bill, Ted, or even Billie or Tesha, you can have an excellent adventure each time you perform a Toastmasters function. By expressing your excellence, you'll help others excel as well.

Extensions of Excellence

When you mentor other members, your excellence speaks through them. Their comportment, the way the carry and express themselves, is a reflection of the way you have mentored them. They can model your excellence through their behavior. My mentor, past International Director Ginger Kane, taught me many lessons in humility, protocol, boundaries and the benefits of advance planning. My expressions of excellence embody these lessons. Now her excellence speaks through me as well as through her own words and deeds.

When you chair a contest or a conference, your excellence is experienced in many ways, from the way the guests are greeted to the fluidity of the event to the way the printed programs, certificates and awards are handled. Expressions aren't just uttered.

Excellence Comes in All Sizes

Don't presume that excellence can only derive from long speaking assignments or when you are the Toastmaster of the day. The best part about expressing your excellence is finding unique means of expression. Here are some expressions of excellence that have inspired me:

- A Division Governor's two-minute report during her District's Business Meeting was action packed. It summarized numerous accomplishments, identified challenges, and recognized Division successes with aplomb and style. It was so good it could have won an impromptu contest!

- Greeters at a contest welcomed every guest so each believed they were the guests of honor.

- A Grammarian went to the extra trouble of defining a few unusual words used that day. While most knew the words in question, not all did. The Grammarian made sure everyone learned.

- A VP-PR took pride in creating fliers and business cards to express the individuality and distinctiveness of her club for the benefit of others.

- A club newsletter editor recognized each member for something noteworthy so they can see their name in print and feel valued for their excellence.

- A member assigned to deliver an opening thought composed a poem about her club in which each member was acknowledged for his or her contributions.

- A VP-Membership pored over the club's rosters from years gone by and sent postcards to former members letting them know they were part of the club's lore and were missed. Each was invited to return, and a number of them did!

Excellence Transcends Toastmasters

Once you set your mind to expressing excellence, you'll excel at doing so. Excellence knows no bounds, within and beyond one's Toastmaster club. Dr. Martin Luther King, Jr. understood the powerful message one's excellence sent to others when he said:

> *"If a man is called to be a street sweeper,*
> *he should sweep streets*
> *even as Michelangelo painted,*
> *or Beethoven played music,*
> *or Shakespeare wrote poetry.*
> *He should sweep streets so well*
> *that all the hosts of heaven and earth*
> *will pause to say,*
> *here lived a great street sweeper*
> *who did his job well."*

Within and beyond Toastmasters you have ample opportunities to express your excellence. Accept the challenge and you will inspire others and yourself to greatness!

Good, Better...Best!

Become the Consummate Toastmaster!

> *"Good, better, best*
> *never let it rest,*
> *until good is better*
> *and better is BEST!"*

Are you a good Toastmaster? Are you striving to be better? How will you become the best Toastmaster that you can be?

Continuous improvement holds the key!

Preparation

GOOD: Showing up on time each week to your club meeting.

BETTER: Showing up to your club meeting a few minutes early each week to help coordinate last minute changes and chat with members informally.

BEST: Showing up early enough to welcome first-time guests at the front door and help your Sergeant-at-Arms set up the meeting room.

In every situation you can be good. In order to be better, you must seek to improve. Yet, to be the best you can be takes a commitment to excellence, a dedication to mastery. And it never ends.

Performance

GOOD: Delivering your speech flawlessly from your script.

BETTER: Delivering your speech expertly, just from an outline.

BEST: Honing the ability to deliver your speech, as intended, with no notes at all.

GOOD: Answering the Table Topic with a cogent response within prescribed time limits.

BETTER: Giving a Table Topic response that has a beginning, middle and end and is also entertaining, educational or thought-provoking.

BEST: Responding in a way that ties into the day's theme, energizes the membership and leaves everyone who heard it touched, moved and inspired!

Best doesn't happen the first time out. Or even the second or third time. But better can! Each time out, you can strive to be better than the last time. When you make that your goal, it becomes foremost in your mind. Best happens over time, through repetition, dedication and diligence.

Continuous Improvement

"After 26 years, I am still learning. I still have areas in which to improve after all these years. Doesn't everybody?" So says

Marion Keibel, DTM, past District 57 Governor and 20-year member of Confidence Builders in Concord, CA (3972-57).

Marion embraces the concept of continuous improvement. Whether she accepts new challenges (like being part of the team rebuilding AdPro (400-57) as a weekly club), or whether she continues to hone her mastery as a speech evaluator, even after winning multiple District evaluation competitions, she always finds room for improvement. And we can too. This is the spirit of *kaizen*, the Japanese concept of continuous improvement. As Toastmasters, when we dedicate ourselves to continuous improvement, we become KTMs—Kaizen Toastmasters.

A Tiger Among Us

Keibel's example of continuously improving as a speech evaluator, even after winning her District's contest, raises the bar for the rest of her District. You see, in any endeavor, to BE the best, you have to BEAT the best! Both Marion and her District competitors improve when they compete head-to-head in their semi-annual contests.

Consider the greatest golfer of our time, Tiger Woods. He is so far ahead of the field, the field has to raise its game just to remain in the hunt. And so they do! They become better to compete against the best. And Tiger benefits from the improving competition and raises his golf game still further.

Whether you strive to be best of class, or strive to achieve your personal best, your quest is never-ending.

Supportiveness

GOOD: You always agree to speak when your name comes up on the agenda scheduler.

BETTER: You also agree when you're asked to be Timekeeper or "Ah" Counter.

BEST: You fill in at one minute to starting time when asked to cover an opening due to a no-show.

This concept of continuous improvement applies to every aspect of our meetings. Consider the role of mentoring.

GOOD: You agree to mentor a new member and invite your mentee to call you whenever he or she has a question.

BETTER: You establish regular opportunities to meet and review the progress of your mentee and answer any questions that arise.

BEST: You not only answer questions posed, but also suggest new opportunities, future roles and additional challenges that you know exist "over the horizon." In this way, you chart a course for their matriculation through the Toastmasters curriculum.

Coaching Others

GOOD: You are praiseworthy in your official evaluation of the speaker at club meetings.

BETTER: You blend praise with recommendations for growth, constructively phrased.

BEST: You blend praise with recommendations, shared publicly, while withholding sensitive suggestions for sharing privately with the speaker.

Sometimes our best efforts are actually found below the waterline. Consider the iceberg. We see the tip of it above the surface. Yet 90% of its mass is found below the waterline where few can see it. As leaders, the public often sees the small percentage of our efforts while the other 90%, our blood, sweat and tears devoted to excellence, is invisible.

Consider all the time and effort that goes into planning a District conference. Rather than judge a conference by how well the conference chair speaks from the platform, consider all the many facets that went into creating the optimal event for everyone.

Planning Events

GOOD: A Fall or Spring District Conference where attendance is high, the business meeting is conducted efficiently, and the conference runs on time.

BETTER: A conference where first-timers want to come back, contests are stirring, keynotes memorable and the Communication and Leadership award winner's speech inspires others.

BEST: A conference in which the standard for excellence is raised, members buzz about it for years (like the 2008 opening ceremonies of the Olympics in Beijing), and the momentum from the conference fuels excellence in the entire District's critical success factors that year and beyond.

Kaizen Complements Toastmastering

Continuous improvement is a concept near and dear to Toastmasters' hearts. We don't just devote a week or month a year to improvement. A third of every meeting is devoted to analyzing what we did well, what we can do better and how we can, as a group, achieve greater results for our club and its members. This, in its essence, is the Japanese concept of Kaizen—continuous improvement.

According to Chuck Reaves, Certified Speaking Professional, CPAE, CSO, and author of *Kaizen for Sales and The NANOSECOND Salesperson*, "Continuous improvement in every endeavor, especially in speaking, is a worthy pursuit. Words are powerful tools that can create, improve or destroy, depending on how effectively they are deployed. As you speak and lead more effectively this year than last, and better next year than this year, your successes will grow resultantly."

Most improvement doesn't come from quantum leaps. It comes from incremental improvements over time. A little better today than yesterday, over time, leads to great improvements, whether in speaking, leading, learning or life.

When you commit to continuous improvement it permeates everything you do and infuses how you live your life. Vow to make each act, each event, each effort your best yet. Then you know, in your heart, that your best is yet to come!

Nine Ways to Improve your Toastmasters Skills

1. **Read!** Read all the Toastmasters literature about how to perform your roles and fulfill the requirements of your positions with the club or District. Read Toastmasters manuals, articles in *Toastmaster* magazine and the handouts created by other Toastmasters. At conventions and conferences, make sure to read and learn from handouts prepared by candidates running from higher office.

2. **Observe!** Watch what successful and veteran Toastmasters do in the performance of their roles. The best make it look effortless or natural, so you may need to look closely. Model your behavior after successful Toastmasters in your club and District.

3. **Brainstorm!** Whether at club officer meetings or during club business meetings, find time to ask "What if…?" or "How can we improve…?" or "What more can I/we do…?" to explore further ways to excel.

4. **Visit other clubs!** You can pick up many ideas from visiting different clubs and observing their procedures, practices and protocols. Collect your own best practices of things you can do individually to be a better Toastmaster.

5. **Attend conventions and conferences!** By attending Toastmasters Leadership Institutes, International Conventions, Regional and District Conferences, you can absorb the best practices of clubs, Districts and Toastmasters from around the world!

6. **Master the curriculum.** Work each speech manual. Embrace Success-Communication, Success-Leadership and the High Performance Leadership program. Earn another CC each year.

7. **Teach.** The act of teaching others helps you formulate what you know, and also allows you to see it through the eyes of others. Whether you lead a Speechcraft or Youth Leadership program, stage a demonstration meeting or form a new club as a sponsor or mentor, your teaching will challenge you to learn more deeply and check your assumptions. From teaching, new insights and growth occurs.

8. **Lead.** When you take a leadership role at the club level or beyond, you take responsibility for events and processes and see them in new lights. You now look for the group instead of just for one. You collaborate with other like-minded leaders on achieving excellence and improving on previous performance.

9. **Experiment.** Try new approaches. Break the mold. Take a periodic risk and be open to new ideas. Use change to your advantage. Remember, our world is changing, and we can change for the better at the same time.

How To Make Miss Manners Proud!

Toastmasters Teaches Timeless Qualities of Politeness, Etiquette and Teamwork

In a manner of speaking, Toastmasters taught me about good manners. While the lessons weren't explicitly laid out in my manuals, I developed sensitivities and good habits that would make Miss Manners proud. You can, too, as you attend your club's meetings each week.

Howdy Stranger: Welcoming Guests

It all started for me even before I joined a club. Club members welcomed me as if I were visiting royalty. They extended themselves to meet and seat me. They helped me feel welcome in this foreign environment by placing an experienced member next to me to anticipate and answer questions I had as a newcomer. Their graciousness contributed to my comfort level and desire to join Toastmasters.

Within a month of joining, I found myself playing the role of gracious host for our guests. Toastmasters was not only helping me get over my fears of greeting strangers, I was now helping strangers feel comfortable. Since the time of Abraham, hospitality has been a revered virtue. In Toastmasters clubs worldwide, the tents of our meeting places are open to all.

Speaking In the Hear and Now

Toastmasters gives us weekly practice in the lost, but well-mannered, art of listening. Communication is best achieved when others listen while one speaks. Toastmasters promotes civil discourse by helping its members improve listening skills and supporting the notion that the speaker alone has the floor while speaking. In a world in which people are constantly interrupting each other, finishing each other's sentences or talking simultaneously, Toastmasters promotes listening skills and polite dialogue. Indeed, if we are ever to get along better, nations and individuals will surely need to improve their ability to listen to each other, and thus better promote understanding.

Punctuality

Toastmasters teaches us the importance of being on time. The meeting starts whether we are there or not. Yet others' roles are often contingent on ours. When we are late, everyone is affected. And most of the civilized world operates on time. Planes and trains depart at their published times. Events such as weddings, symphony and opera performances and movies all occur on schedule. In life, polite people show up on time or early and are prepared to play their roles. Toastmasters sets a wonderful example in helping its members to be on time and respect time limits. We start on time, run on time and end on time!

Trust!

Every week, when we sign up to fulfill a role, others count on us. By honoring our commitment we're building our reputation.

When we "are" our word and do the things we say we'll do, others build trust in us. Each of us has made a tacit agreement to assist the team, help the club and honor our role for the week. Toastmasters helps us become a person others can count on, a person who honors his or her word and who can be depended upon. Toastmasters helps us stand for something: good manners!

Teamwork

I grew up as an only child. I grew accustomed to only caring for myself. Yet when I joined my Toastmasters club, suddenly I began to think in terms of twenty, not just one! When I was the week's Toastmaster and created the agenda, I made 20 copies. When, as WordMaster, I introduced a word of the week, I printed it in letters big enough to be seen at the back of the room so all twenty members could read it with ease.

Toastmaster membership helps us think in terms of every club member's success. In 1995-96, past District 57 Governor Jim Doyle, Jr.'s theme was TEAM: TOGETHER EVERYONE ACHIEVES MORE. Indeed, Toastmasters helps us succeed as a club, Area, Division and a District, as well as individually. What a wonderful quality to cultivate. In a world that is increasingly intertwined, teamwork is more and more essential to our individual and collective success. In its own way Toastmasters promotes teamwork for the betterment of all.

Appreciating Others

Ultimately, the Toastmasters experience is about achieving success. When we succeed, others revel in our accomplishments. More often, we support, recognize and appreciate others' successes. To be a Toastmaster is to be magnanimous in our praise of others. Toastmasters taught me to see and appreciate the efforts of others and shine the light of praise upon them. My focus shifted from myself to others through my Toastmasters experience.

The essence of manners is steeped in courtesy for others. When I acknowledge members by their name, rank, educational accomplishments and contributions to our club, I see them more fully. They are more than someone who speaks before or after me, they are the sum of many skills, accomplishments, contributions and qualities. By giving them their due, I demonstrate graciousness and appreciation. That's what well-mannered people do!

Honing My Humility

One of the best lessons I learned in Toastmasters is how praise I receive can be shared with others. Indeed, it's polite to accept thanks and praise with humility. When I share my own recognition, others too get to bask in the spotlight. I've come to prefer the sharing of success in this way.

The Power of Politeness

Dana May Casperson, author of *Power Etiquette*, said, "The skills one learns through Toastmasters—listening, punctuality, trust, teamwork, appreciating others—are the same skills that help you succeed in the workplace."

Dana May's POWER ETIQUETTE GROUP has observed a general decline in etiquette with the advent of many technology tools. She also sees the edge Toastmasters carry when they compete for jobs and promotions in the workplace. "You learn, practice and hone a set of skills in Toastmasters that is transferable to social relationships and professional commitments beyond Toastmasters. They become a part of your life."

Four hundred years ago, British clergyman and author Thomas Fuller (1608-1661) rightly recognized that "all doors open to courtesy." Today, I submit that the Toastmasters experience opens us all to the way to be courteous and polite and to work well together.

As you're toasted for your Toastmastering, harness the power of politeness, utilize the etiquette edge and make Miss Manners proud. Here's to YOU!

Becoming the *Consummate Toastmaster*

Consummate: Supremely accomplished or skilled.

To the outside world, you—as Toastmaster—are expected to propose toasts upon demand. Within Toastmasters, there are well prescribed milestones of Toastmasters achievement. You are encouraged to attain achievements such as the CC, AC, CL and AL upon completion of manuals, roles and responsibilities.

Yet to really become *The Consummate Toastmaster*, there are certain skills that aren't necessarily emphasized in manuals or taught at conferences and leadership institutes. The Consummate Toastmaster possesses special skills he or she can apply at any time, within or beyond Toastmasters. Regardless of rank or title, you, too, can become *The Consummate Toastmaster*.

Hip Check

For instance, can you give what is referred to as a hip- or back-pocket speech? Many a Toastmaster can give a speech with a week's preparation time to write, rehearse and deliver well-chosen words in cogent fashion. Yet what about situations where the featured speaker cancels at the last minute? Or at work when the scheduled speaker falls sick or is stuck in transit. *The Consummate Toastmaster* can give a speech on short notice. Can you?

The *Elevator* Speech

Perhaps the most important speech you ever make to benefit your club may, ironically, be given outside the club. Can you give an elevator speech—a mini-speech to a stranger—extolling the virtues of your club so strangers see fit to join you? This sixteen-second sound bite is a powerful tool for sharing the magic of your club with strangers. No timing lights will tell you if you've spoken too long, but if the listener asks for more information about attending your next club meeting, you know you've aced this speech!

Your elevator speech is just as important, or more important, beyond Toastmasters when meeting new contacts, breaking the ice, becoming visible and extending your professional network. It's how you become known to others and begin building business relationships. Learn to push the right buttons with your elevator speech.

Introductions

The gateway to new relationships, the introduction, is a skill Toastmasters can and should master. Done effectively, all parties feel valued, special and welcomed. Use your club meetings, and the time before and after the gavel sounds, to introduce yourself to strangers, introduce guests to your club's leadership, and draw guests out of their shy shells.

A club that prides itself on effective introductions in meetings is one whose members know, respect and like each other. That's a club I want to be a part of! You bring the world closer together when you use your communication skills to introduce people to each other. THIS is how to build your social network!

And don't just stop once the meeting ends. Use your skills and confidence outside of Toastmasters to introduce yourself to others and new contacts to your associates. Flex your communication muscles through powerful introductions.

Under Construction But *Not* Under-Constructive

We know well the power of positive thinking. Don't underestimate the power of positive speaking. When your speech evaluation is positive, it encourages the speaker, gives her or him hope and provides a place to grow from. When you are cutting, harsh or otherwise negative, you mute the growth of your colleague and send a chill throughout your club.

The Consummate Toastmaster can deliver praise and possibilities for improvement in a positive fashion. It's easy to bash others and denigrate their efforts. A true Toastmaster can even deliver criticism in a positive manner. Furthermore, your positive evaluation signals to other members and guests that your club is a safe haven for speaking and sharing.

In the work world, your evaluation prowess will also allow you to praise and support others, even while helping them improve through constructive feedback.

Humility

The many programs of Toastmasters are full of opportunities to receive accolades and recognition for accomplishments. Upon completion of speeches, manuals and roles, it's not uncommon to be bestowed with applause, verbal praise, pins, plaques, ribbons and certificates, to say nothing of awards for winning contests.

Learning to graciously accept praise and kind words with humility is a virtue. In life there are winners and there are whiners. Learning to win is good. Learning humility is priceless. Become as gracious in victory as in defeat. And share the light you received with others. Who mentored you? Who coached you? Who helped you along the way? Remember, success has many parents! Find and acknowledge yours.

You even create a more generous work environment when you display the same humility and grace beyond Toastmasters. *The Consummate Toastmaster* is classy.

A Resource to Others

Outside of Toastmasters we're surrounded by others who are petrified at the prospect of giving a speech or even speaking in public. *The Consummate Toastmaster* avails him or herself to colleagues, co-workers and friends to coach them when it's their turn to speak. Whether at conferences, departmental meetings, formal or informal office gatherings, they have fear and you have formulae. *The Consummate Toastmaster* coaches non-speakers how to construct and deliver appropriate remarks without stage fright. Of course, *The Consummate Toastmaster* then invites these non-Toastmasters to join his or her club for ongoing skill-building opportunities.

A Master of Improv

Toastmasters teaches you leadership. Table Topics teaches you to think on your feet. *The Consummate Toastmaster* blends these two to become an improvisational leader. You see a need, you address it. You see a vacant role…you fill it. Others need help… you provide it. You lead and live in the moment, ever available to fill in, speak out, step up or otherwise lead or assist others.

The Consummate Toastmaster is proactive. And others appreciate it! Open the door, hold the bus, help the infirm cross the street… whatever the need, *The Consummate Toastmaster* fills the void to save the day!

Lifelong Learners

True Toastmasters never cease to learn and improve. They keep working and reworking their manuals, continue to attend meetings dutifully, and contribute to leadership institutes and conferences. Why? Because they're lifelong learners. It's how they enact the value of continuous improvement.

Consummate Toastmasters are STARs!

Well-rounded Toastmasters are STARs: they Speak, Teach, Achieve and Recognize the efforts and successes of others. STARs flex each of their Toastmasters muscles to make a difference in their club and District, community and our world at large. Use your skills and be the STAR you were destined to be. Then, people will regard you as *The Consummate Toastmaster!*

VI. NEXT STEPS

Congratulations! You have become a Consummate Toastmaster. This is quite a milestone even if there isn't a pin or plaque to accompany it.

Of course, you know that every milestone becomes a stepping stone to further accomplishment. The question for you is what's next? Now, what will you do? How will you apply your masterful communication and leadership skills, your hard-earned Toastmasters experience, to make a difference in the world?

Read on, to learn how to extend your sphere of influence and shape our world!

What Now?

The World Awaits You and Your Communication and Leadership Skills!

Congratulations on achieving your DTM, and winning a speech contest and starting a new club. Your home club is proud of you. Your District honors you. You bring pride to your family and friends. To which I add: What now? While there is much more to do within Toastmasters, it's time to consider how you will simultaneously share "the new you" with the world.

What will you do *next*?

Toastmasters provides a nurturing environment where you constantly learn new skills and polish existing ones. It's a most supportive learning laboratory where you experiment, grow and flex your communication and leadership skills. As such, it's a magnificent staging area for success. But sooner or later, it's time to apply your new skill set in the outside world.

Where will you go from here? Where will you apply your communication and leadership skills? How will you utilize the expertise, confidence and experience accrued in Toastmasters to shape our world?

Make no mistake, the world awaits! The need has never been greater for reliable leaders and confident, credible communicators to step forward. It's time you take your rightful place among the shapers and achievers of our world.

Toastmasters Leads to Success

Before making the TV show *Home Improvement*, movie and TV star Tim Allen sought self-improvement through Toastmasters. In fact, many successful people from all walks of life have benefited from Toastmasters. You're in esteemed company.

It may be a cliché to say that only the sky is the limit when participating in Toastmasters. But James Lovell, John Young and the late Walter Schirra were three Toastmasters who didn't let the sky limit them. You probably recognize them as NASA Astronauts who've orbited the Earth from outer space. You never know how far Toastmasters can take you.

Toastmasters: The People's Choice!

Former Toastmasters have found their way into the highest levels of leadership in many countries. Did you know the former Premier of British Columbia, William Bennett, was a Toastmaster? As was Ben Couch, a Member of Parliament in New Zealand. In the United States, former US Senators John V. Tunney and Sam Nunn, and former Speaker of the House of Representatives Carl Albert were all Toastmasters, as was Missouri Congresswoman Carol Stoker.

Linda Lingle is a Competent Toastmaster. She is also the Governor of the State of Hawai'i. Lingle said, "Toastmasters helps members organize their thoughts and express them in a way that can move people to action." She added that, as a member of the Toastmasters organization, she learned valuable lessons that have helped her "articulate ideas in a clear and compelling fashion."

Given your own lessons learned and confidence gleaned, what ideas will you put forth? Who will you move to action?

Be Heard Now!

Communication and leadership skills can propel you into local, regional or national office. The abilities to persuade, serve, lead and listen allow you to mobilize others, enlist them in your vision and champion their issues. Whether you bring your Toastmaster skills to town meetings, council meetings or join task forces, commissions or other committees, you can shape your community and beyond through rolling up your sleeves, speaking and leading.

In Every Profession…

The world is full of Toastmasters who have made a difference in sports, politics, business, social movements and elsewhere. What's more, skills and confidence cultivated in Toastmasters presents professionals with options. They can migrate from their initial field of expertise into new or different areas.

The Man with the Golden Tongue

Did you know the founder of the National Speakers Association, Cavett Robert, was a Toastmaster for over 60 years? Robert was runner-up in Toastmasters' 1941 speech contest. After coming in second place, Toastmasters founder, Dr. Ralph C. Smedley, coached Robert to develop a signature story. Dr. Smedley told

Robert, "If you had given a story, a signature story, I believe you would have won." The next year, Cavett did win what is now known as Toastmasters' World Championship of Public Speaking.

And what, you ask, did Cavett Robert do for an encore? In 1973, he incorporated the National Speakers Association. Today, NSA boasts 3,625 members, many of whom were, and remain, Toastmasters. Each, in turn, inspires thousands through their speeches, training and leadership. Included among NSA membership are many recent World Champions of Public Speaking.

The 2008 World Champion of Public Speaking, LaShunda Rundles, from Dallas, Texas, is a lupus survivor. She desires to speak on behalf of other patients for the Lupus Foundation of America. Her winning speech titled "Speak!" encourages people to use their voices to change the world.

Robert's influence lives on in current generations of speakers. Rundles and other speakers now have a greater platform with which to transform our world. What cause will you champion?

Hill Climbing

Dr. Napoleon Hill, author of the best-seller *Think and Grow Rich*, was also a Toastmaster. Regarded as the founder of the science of success, Hill grew up in poverty and rose up to be a presidential advisor in the United States. Along the way, he interviewed 500 millionaires to ascertain their secrets to success.

Hill said, "If you do not conquer self, you will be conquered by self." For Hill, self-confidence was derived from Toastmasters. The self-confident Hill influenced millions through his speaking and writing. His thoughts are as valid today on the application of skills developed along the way. He said, "You must get involved to have an impact. No one is impressed with the won-lost record of the referee." The lesson for us all: It's time to get onto the field and into the game.

Athletes Achieve On and Off the Field

Successful athletes with communication and leadership skills honed in Toastmasters can effectively transition to post-sports roles as commentators, coaches and more. Professional football player George Atkinson was a defensive back and punt returner for Coach John Madden's Oakland Raiders in the 1970's. After winning Super Bowl XI in 1977, and later retiring from the NFL, George joined a specialty Toastmasters club focusing on television broadcasting. Now he is a Raiders pre- and post-game announcer and host of their BEHIND THE SHIELD television show.

What Now?

You're no longer the shy, tentative speaker or leader who joined Toastmasters. Your esteem has soared. You relish opportunities to speak and lead. To confine both speaking and leading to your club or District is to underutilize the skills you've cultivated. To be all you can be in Toastmasters, it's time to apply your skills beyond Toastmasters. The world awaits! It's time you answer for yourself the question: What now?

Taking It To The Streets!

Five ways to leverage Toastmasters to impact your world:

1. Conduct a Youth Leadership Program for a local school or worthy youth group

2. Conduct a Speechcraft for a retirement center or other local group.

3. Deliver Success-Communication or Success-Leadership programs for the general public as a service to the community

4. Volunteer your speech evaluation skills to local Lions clubs for their annual student youth contests

5. As a High Performance Leadership project, partner with your community college to create a program on communication and leadership

Ten Ways to apply Toastmasters skills in your World:

1. Join a political campaign.

2. Run for public office.

3. Apply to speak on behalf of your favorite non-profit.

4. Become a leader in your local chamber of commerce.

5. Become a block leader in your neighborhood.

6. Join your neighborhood association.

7. Launch a cable-access TV show.

8. Write Op-Ed page columns for your local newspaper.

9. Stage an event or coordinate a function for your organization, community or religious institution.

10. Coach, teach or train youth, during or after school.

Good Luck!

VII. ABOUT THE AUTHOR:
Craig's Toastmasters Story

Prior to joining Toastmasters in 1992, Craig Harrison was a mumbling, stumbling, bumbling communicator with low self-esteem. Today he is a professional speaker with a worldwide reputation. He owes it all to Toastmasters! They turned his fear into fun and enabled him to go from free to fee as a speaker.

Harrison joined Lakeview Toastmasters in Oakland, California in July, 1992. By July, 1996 he simultaneously became a Distinguished Toastmaster (DTM) and District 57 Governor, for over 100 coastal Northern California clubs. Whether as a Club President, Area or Division Governor, Lieutenant Governor or Toastmasters Ambassador without portfolio, Craig has inspired, entertained and mentored clubs and members worldwide.

Craig has started clubs, saved clubs, written prolifically for *Toastmaster* magazine, written and been quoted about Toastmasters for the *Wall Street Journal, San Francisco Chronicle* and numerous other publications. Among the clubs Craig has helped form: Urban League Toastmasters, LaughLovers, Speakers Forum, Pro-Toasties, Heart2Heart, Rockridge and a dozen more.

Craig has spoken at multiple Toastmasters International Conventions, Regional and District Conferences and trained others through Toastmasters Leadership Institutes in various districts. He's spoken to clubs in Australia, The People's Republic of China, Japan, Canada and throughout the United States.

Harrison received a presidential citation from Toastmasters International in Reno, NV in 2004.

Craig's Professional Story

Craig Harrison began his public speaking career as an eleven year old when he went door-to-door in his hometown of Berkeley CA, selling Used Jokes. He's been connecting to strangers ever since!

As an adult, Craig has worked for corporations and non-profits as a manager, director, curriculum developer, editor, desktop publisher and sports coach. He's spent a decade in high-tech, worked in publishing, health care and with youth. He's coached sports domestically and internationally. As a leader beyond Toastmasters he's chaired the board of a listener-sponsored FM radio station and been a leader with the National Speakers Association, Storytelling Association of California, American Society for Training and Development and the International Customer Service Association.

The adult Craig Harrison is a professional speaker, trainer and communication coach who founded Expressions of Excellence!™ to help professionals express their excellence. Craig builds credible and confident communicators and inspires stellar sales and service organizations.

You've read about Craig in the *Wall Street Journal, Financial Times of London,* and *Business Week.* He's been interviewed by 60 MINUTES, appeared on BBC RADIO and has been quoted in *Selling Power, Support World, Real Simple, Orange County Register, Executive Excellence* and *Customer Communicator.*

Craig is the author of CULTIVATING THE LEADER IN YOU, the popular customer service tips booklet STELLAR SERVICE! and his tips booklet *Your Sixteen Second Success: Ride Your Elevator*

Speech to Success! even inspired a week's worth of panels of the comic strip Sally Forth! Additional learning tools are available at his website: www.ExpressionsOfExcellence.com/products.html.

His clients include Hilton Hotels, United Airlines, the U.S. Army, Salvation Army, AT&T, Pfizer, multiple University of California campuses, nolo.com, the Go Green Initiative Association, MPI, NSA, CAPS, eWomenNetwork, BNI and numerous associations and institutions. A client list may be found at www.expressionsofexcellence.com/client_list.html.

* * * * * * * * * * * *

Grow your Toastmasters learning library with other offerings of Craig's:

(This book)

CULTIVATING THE LEADER IN YOU!

This pocketbook on leadership helps emerging and aspiring leaders speak, think and act as leaders. Containing 101 leadership tips, "next steps" and an action plan, it's ideal for new managers, board members and makes a great gift for new graduates. **Cost: $10**

STELLAR SERVICE! 101 Top Drawer Customer Service Tips for Bottom Line Success:

Customer service tips for face-to-face, telephone and Internet-based customer service. How to handle problems, infuse excellence, sharpen quality, win and keep customers and so much more. An ideal tips booklet to begin or maintain stellar training and service standards.
Cost:..$10

Electronic Copies...Price Inclusive
Hard Copies: Add $2 Shipping & Handling <u>Per item</u>.
Pay by Cash or Credit Cards

www.ExpressionsOfExcellence/products.html

Become A *Passionate* Toastmaster!

From Free to Fee
A 40-page special report for Toastmasters and all aspiring professional speakers! It teaches you how to specialize, market, obtain platform mastery. Learn to be audience-centered, customize, leverage you local surroundings and much, much more.
E-Book Report: $30
Hard Copy Report: $30 + S/H

From Free to Fee:
On Becoming A Professional Speaker
<u>Craig's 45-pg. Special Report *Plus* 8 Bonus Reports:</u>

- ❖ How to Be Audience-Centered
- ❖ Cold Calling for Speakers
- ❖ Customizing Presentations
- ❖ Customer Service for Speakers
- ❖ Ice-Breakers for Speakers & Trainers
- ❖ Dealing with Difficult Questioners
- ❖ Elevator Speeches for Speakers

- ❖ Humor & When To Use It
- ❖ Find Your Speaking Topic
- ❖ Bypassing Gatekeepers...

CD: $60

193

Become A Money Speaker!

This Special Report consists of eight targeted guides addressing key aspects of transitioning from a free public speaker to a professional speaker who commands high fees and is a thought-leader providing great value to clients. This report helps you with marketing, platform skills and professional development. Topics include:

- ❖ Finding Your Topic As A Paid Speaker
- ❖ Being Audience-Centered
- ❖ Customizing
- ❖ Use of Ice-Breakers
- ❖ Humor, how to use it and how not to!
- ❖ Dealing with Difficult Audiences and Situations
- ❖ Elevator Speeches for Speakers
- ❖ Cold Calling for Speakers
- ❖ Sales through Storytelling for Speakers
- ❖ Customer Service for Speakers

**Cost: $49.99 Hard Copy of E-Book.
Available at:
www.ExpressionsOfExcellence.com/products.html**

Become A *Passionate* Toastmaster!

Accelerate your Growth with Coaching

Whether you are:

- ❖ A new Toastmaster who wants to maximize your Toastmasters experience
- ❖ An aspiring or emerging professional speaker
- ❖ Transitioning from Speaker to Trainer
- ❖ A District Leader seeking President's Distinguished status
- ❖ A business professional seeking to Fast-Track your learning
- ❖ Motivated to form your own corporate, community or specialty club

Or have other visions of grandeur, I can help!

I've coached as well as trained *hundreds* of Toastmasters… speakers, leaders, contestants and mentors, as well as professional speakers, managers, directors and leaders at all levels.

In person or telephone coaching can catapult you to new heights, hold you accountable and cut months or years off your learning curve. Learn from one who has truly been there and done all there is to do in Toastmasters.

**Call (510) 547-0664 today or e-mail Craig for a free consultation:
Craig@ExpressionsOfExcellence.com**